Children's
Great Explorers
Encyclopedia

Author: Simon Adams

Consultant: Philip Parker

This edition produced by Tall Tree Ltd, London

First published by Parragon in 2008
Parragon
Queen Street House
4 Queen Street
Bath BA1 1HE, UK

ISBN 978-1-4075-1645-5

Printed in Malaysia

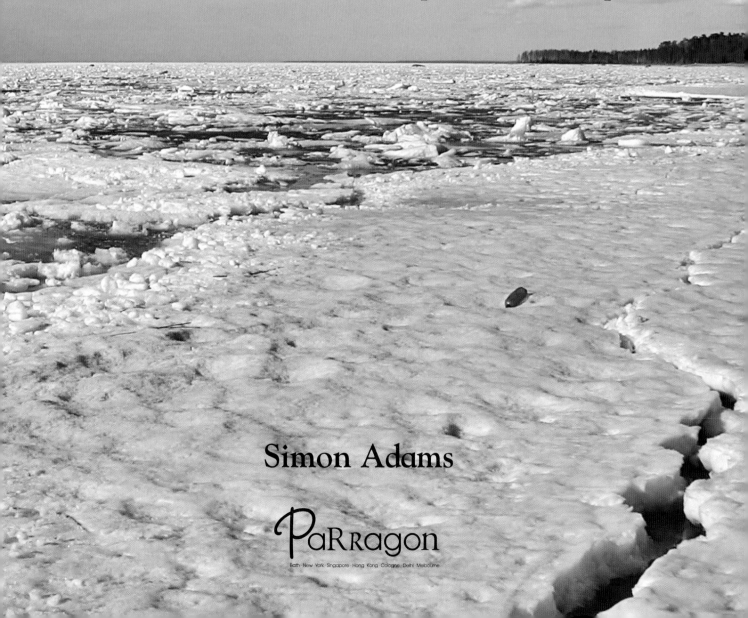

Children's
Great Explorers
Encyclopedia

Discover the world in the footsteps of famous explorers

Simon Adams

PaRragon

Bath · New York · Singapore · Hong Kong · Cologne · Delhi · Melbourne

Greenland

Hudson
Bay

Labrador
Sea

North
America

Atlantic Ocean

N

NW   NE

W   E

SW

SE

S

CONTENTS

EARLY EXPLORERS   9
Egyptian and Phoenician traders • Ancient Greeks
Viking settlers • Muslim travelers • Chinese Buddhists

EUROPE LOOKS EAST   35
Sailing around Africa • Trade with India • Christians on
a mission • Mapping Siberia • Tackling the deserts

A NEW ROUTE TO ASIA   61
Christopher Columbus • A western course to Asia • Finding
a new continent • Braving the Arctic • Opening up Japan

SAILING AROUND THE WORLD   87
Around South America • Pirates and adventurers
Non-stop voyages • Charting the oceans • Going solo

THE NEW WORLD   113
Spanish conquistadors • Searching for gold • Pushing into
the north • Trading with the Indians • The Wild West frontier

THE PACIFIC AND AUSTRALIA   139
Polynesian explorers • Europeans in the South Seas
Finding Antarctica • Crossing Australia • Retracing the past

INTO AFRICA   165
Following the great rivers • The mystery of the Sahara
The African Great Lakes • In search of Dr Livingstone

EXTREME EXPLORATION   191
The race to the Poles • The world beneath the waves
Conquering Everest • Into Space • Reaching the Moon

GLOSSARY AND TIME LINE   216

INDEX   220

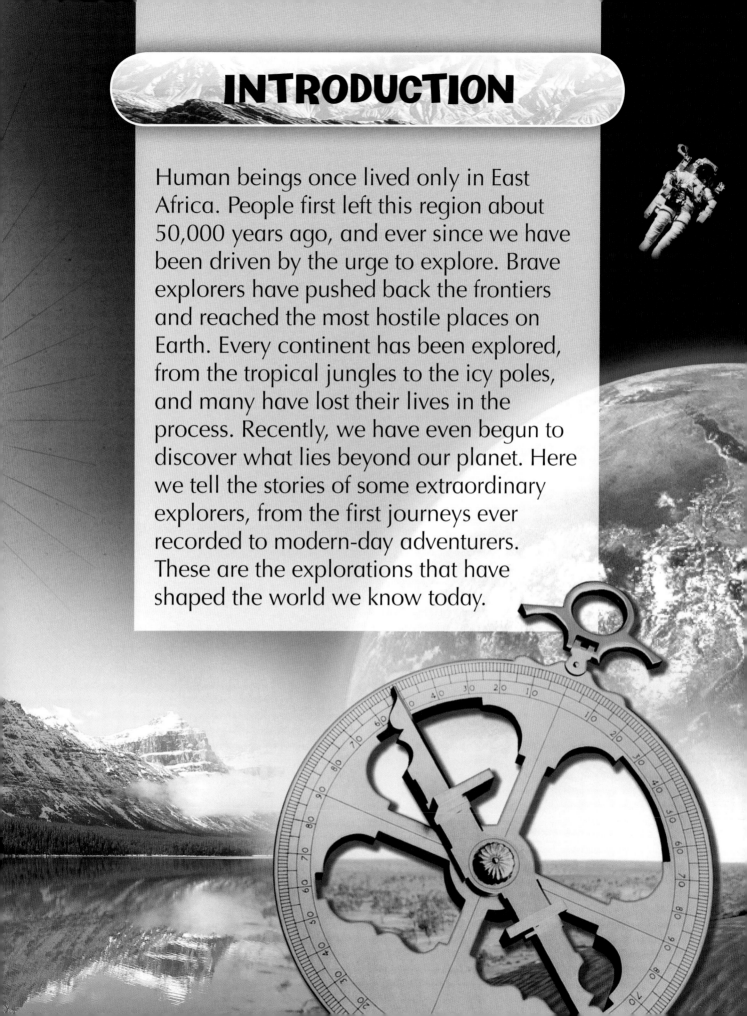

INTRODUCTION

Human beings once lived only in East Africa. People first left this region about 50,000 years ago, and ever since we have been driven by the urge to explore. Brave explorers have pushed back the frontiers and reached the most hostile places on Earth. Every continent has been explored, from the tropical jungles to the icy poles, and many have lost their lives in the process. Recently, we have even begun to discover what lies beyond our planet. Here we tell the stories of some extraordinary explorers, from the first journeys ever recorded to modern-day adventurers. These are the explorations that have shaped the world we know today.

EARLY EXPLORERS

The first travelers all set out on their journeys for a reason. The Egyptians, Phoenicians, and Greeks traveled for trade. The Chinese left home to look for new allies or to find out more about their religion. The Norsemen set sail in search of new places to live. We know about these early adventurers because some of them kept records and wrote about their journeys, which took them to the very edges of their known world.

Voyage to Punt

We do not know the name of the first explorer. However, we do know that the ancient Egyptians undertook a voyage to a place called Punt about 3,500 years ago, during the reign of Queen Hatshepsut.

By land and sea

After making contact with the people of Punt, the Egyptians traveled there in order to trade. We do not know where Punt was, but it may have been in northern Somalia, at the end of the Red Sea. The Egyptians dragged all the materials they needed to build their ships overland from the Nile River to the Red Sea coast. There they built five ships and sailed south for a year.

Queen Hatshepsut

Hatshepsut ruled Egypt around 1473–1458 B.C. She was often portrayed in statues as a man. This is because it was almost unheard of at the time for a woman to become a pharaoh (Egyptian ruler).

Hatshepsut's temple

Hatshepsut built a huge temple in which to protect her body when she died. The temple is built into cliffs on the west bank of the Nile River at Thebes, one of the main religious centers of Egypt.

Carvings on the temple walls tell us about the voyage to Punt.

The riches of Punt

Once in Punt, the Egyptians loaded their ships with myrrh trees, incense, ivory, ebony, gold, leopard skins, and other luxuries. They also took live animals with them, such as baboons and pet dogs. Once their ships were full, they sailed north again up the Red Sea. They crossed over land once more to the Nile River and sailed home.

Hatshepsut's temple walls depict the triumphant return of the sailors from Punt.

Time Line

c.2500 B.C.
Ancient Egyptians first make contact with Punt

c.1473 B.C.
Hatshepsut rules on behalf of her infant stepson Thutmose III

c.1470 B.C.
Hatshepsut orders the voyage to Punt to bring back precious items for her temples and palaces

c.1458 B.C.
Hatshepsut dies

It's Amazing!

An inscription in the temple states that "Never was the like brought to any monarch since the world began."

Egyptian ships

The trading ships of ancient Egypt were made of short planks of wood tied together with rope around a basic wooden frame. The ships had one large linen sail and up to 16 oars on either side to propel them when the wind was light or in the wrong direction. A large oar at the back was used for steering.

The trading ships had plenty of room inside to store the items traded in Punt.

Phoenician traders

The Phoenicians, a people from Lebanon, on the east coast of the Mediterranean Sea, established colonies where they could trade with the local people. One of these colonies was Carthage in North Africa.

The voyage of Hanno

Around 475 B.C., one trader, Hanno, led a fleet of 60 ships out of Carthage to search for new places to establish colonies. They sailed out of the Mediterranean and down the coast of Africa. Along the way they saw a volcano erupting. They may have sailed as far as Mt. Cameroon, which is the only volcano on the west coast.

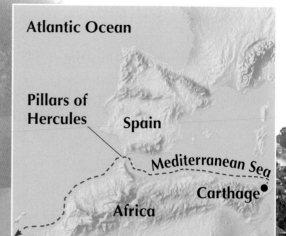

The Pillars of Hercules marked the end of the known world.

Pillars of Hercules

As Hanno and his fleet headed west, they passed between the Pillars of Hercules. These two rocks are thought to have been the Rock of Gibraltar on the European coast and Mt. Hacho on the African coast.

It's Amazing!

Hanno records meeting people covered with hair, whom he called "Gorillas."

Phoenician ships may have looked like this.

Phoenician ships

We don't know much about Phoenician trading ships because records about them lack any technical details. They were probably made of wood planks and powered with a single sail and rows of oars on either side.

The color purple

The Phoenicians were famous for their fine purple cloth. They extracted a liquid from sea snails to make the dye. For a pound of dye, up to 60,000 snails were needed, so purple cloth was very expensive.

Purple cloth was so rare that it was only worn by the very rich.

These ruins in present-day Tunisia are almost all that is left of the great city of Carthage.

Time Line

c.814 B.C.
Phoenicians establish trading city Carthage in North Africa

c.600 B.C.
A Phoenician ship sails around Africa

c.475 B.C.
Hanno sails down the west coast of Africa

Around Africa

Hanno was not the first Phoenician traveler. In around 600 B.C., the Egyptian pharaoh Necho II hired a Phoenician crew to sail down the Red Sea, around Africa, and then back through the Mediterranean to Egypt. The voyage took three years because the crew stopped each year to plant and reap a harvest of food.

Around Britain

The ancient Greeks were great traders and explorers. In 330 B.C. a Greek merchant, Pytheas, made one of the most remarkable voyages of the ancient world.

Time Line

c.600 B.C.
Greeks establish colony of Massilia

c.380 B.C.
Pytheas born

c.330–320 B.C.
Pytheas voyages around Britain and visits Thule. He records his voyage in *On the Ocean*, a book that is later lost

c.310 B.C.
Pytheas dies

Pytheas

Pytheas was born around 380 B.C. in Massilia, a Greek colony in southern France, known today as Marseilles. During his voyage, he was the first to describe the aurora borealis, or northern lights, the glowing green sky that sometimes occurs in the far north.

It's Amazing!

Tin from Cornwall, England, was taken at low tide to the island of St. Michael's Mount. The merchants who bought it were scared to go to the mainland because the locals were so fierce!

To Thule

Pytheas set out from Massilia through the Mediterranean. He followed the Atlantic coastline north until he crossed the English Channel to Cornwall in England. Here, he saw miners extracting and refining tin into fist-sized ingots. He then sailed north up the Irish Sea and through the Hebrides to the Orkney Islands north of Scotland. From here, he sailed north for a further six days until he sighted Thule, "the most distant of all the lands."

Thule may have been Iceland, below, but we cannot know for sure.

Thule

We do not know where Thule was, but Pytheas said that the sun never set there and the sea was transformed into a material "on which it was neither possible to walk nor to sail"—ice. This suggests Thule was close to the Arctic Ocean.

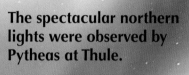

The spectacular northern lights were observed by Pytheas at Thule.

The Greeks made goods to trade, such as this necklace.

Greek trade

The ancient Greeks founded many colonies around the Mediterranean and Black seas. These colonies grew rich by trading tin, grain, and other raw materials in return for Greek goods, such as wine and jewelry.

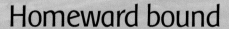

Homeward bound

At Thule, Pytheas turned back south, exploring the east coast of Britain and then crossing the North Sea to the Amber Islands off the coast of Denmark. From there, he returned to Massilia, probably by sailing up the Rhine River and then traveling across land to sail down the Rhone River to the coast.

In defense of China

In 138 B.C., the Chinese Empire was under threat from the Huns, a nomadic tribe from central Asia. In response, the Chinese emperor Wudi sent one of his officials to seek allies among neighboring states.

The futile search

Zhang Qian set out from the Chinese capital, Chang'an, with a plan to enlist the help of the Yuezhi tribe of central Asia. But before reaching them, he was captured by the Huns and imprisoned for ten years. When he finally escaped, he traveled east to Ferghana, where he met the Yue-chi. However, they refused to fight the Huns, so Zhang Qian returned home empty-handed.

Time Line

c.160 B.C.
Birth of Zhang Qian

138–127 B.C.
Zhang Qian seeks an alliance with the Yue-chi but is imprisoned by the Huns

126 B.C.
Zhang returns home

119 B.C.
Zhang's second journey to central Asia

107 B.C.
Zhang Qian dies

c.100 B.C.
The Silk Road opens

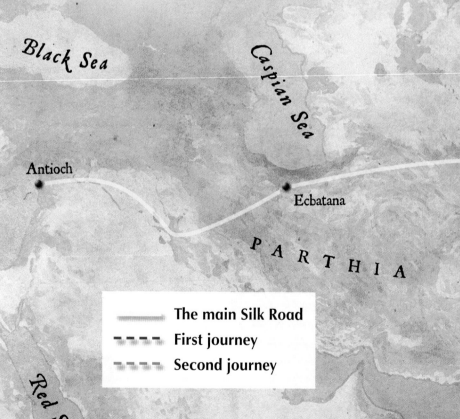
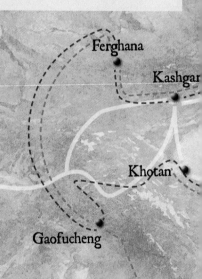

Black Sea

Caspian Sea

Ferghana

Kashgar

Antioch

Merv

Khotan

Ecbatana

Gaofucheng

P A R T H I A

The main Silk Road

First journey

Second journey

I N D I A

Red Sea

Arabian Sea

The Han made sophisticated ceramics, such as this, one of the prized Ferghana horses.

Han Dynasty

The Han Dynasty of emperors ruled China from 206 B.C. until A.D. 220. The emperors believed their great power came from heaven. They governed the country through a series of powerful land-owning families. They also built up a large army and extended their empire to cover much of modern-day China.

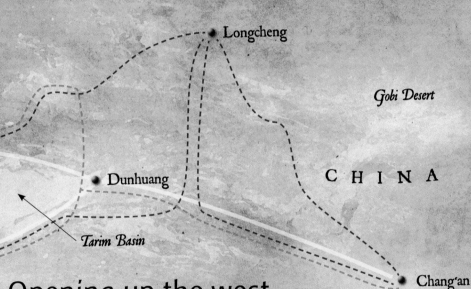

Opening up the west

The emperor was very interested in Zhang Qian's reports of the people who lived to the west of his borders. Around 116 B.C., Wudi sent Zhang Qian back to meet these people again. This time he had more success. He made useful contacts and explored the trade routes that linked China with Kashgar and Ferghana, and south into India.

What Next?

Zhang Qian's report to the emperor led to the opening of the Silk Road, a new trade route to Parthia and the Roman Empire. The Silk Road remained the main trade route between China and Europe for many centuries.

In search of Buddha

Buddhism reached China from India in about A.D. 70, but contact between the two countries was restricted by the Himalaya Mountains that separated them. Two Chinese monks traveled to India to find out more about their religion.

Faxian the monk

In A.D. 399, Faxian set out from China and traveled west along the Silk Road to Khotan in the far west, where he found many Buddhist monks. He then headed south across the mountains into India, where he studied in the Buddhist monasteries along the Ganges River. After further stops in Sri Lanka, Malaya, and Indonesia, he returned home in A.D. 412 with manuscripts and sacred objects.

There are many giant statues of Buddha, such as this one in south Asia.

These Burmese monks live a simple life as they follow the teachings of Buddha.

Buddhism

Buddha was born in northern India in 485 B.C. He taught that people could overcome suffering and hardship in the world by becoming enlightened and reaching a state of supreme happiness. From India, Buddhism spread into Tibet, China, Korea, and Japan, and south to Sri Lanka and southeast Asia.

Time Line

c. a.d. 337
Birth of Faxian

a.d. 399–412
Faxian travels to India

a.d. 422
Death of Faxian

c. a.d. 602
Xuanzang born

a.d. 629–645
Xuanzang travels to India via central Asia

a.d. 664
Xuanzang dies

Xuanzang

Xuanzang was born in a.d. 602 and left for India when he was 27. He was anxious to explain the difficult teachings he found in Buddhist texts. By the time he returned home, 16 years later, he had collected over 650 religious books.

Xuanzang carried his books on his back.

The ancient scholar

In a.d. 629, the monk Xuanzang set out to India to study the old Buddhist texts. He learned the ancient Indian language of Sanskrit and traveled around the country, finding out about Buddha and his teachings. His journal describes the approximately 40,000 miles (60,000 km) he traveled. It became an important source of information on the geography of India and China.

What Next?

The Chinese invented a method of printing blocks of text onto paper around the a.d. 500s so that more people could read the new Buddhist texts.

Man of letters

Faxian's name means "Illustrious master of the Law," because he was a smart Buddhist scholar. We know little about his life other than what he recorded in his book, *A Record of Buddhistic Kingdoms*.

The Ajanta monastery in India was carved out of rock around the time of Faxian's travels.

The Norsemen

We often think of the Norsemen, or Vikings, as savage raiders, looting and pillaging. But the Norsemen were also intrepid travelers and traders. They were the first Europeans to visit North America.

Leif Erikson

Around A.D. 1000, Leif Erikson visited North America, sailing from Greenland down the coast of Labrador. He reached a place he named Vinland (Wine-land) because of its wild berries.

Setting sail

We are not sure why in the 9th century A.D. the Norsemen decided to leave home. However, it is likely that the growing number of younger sons with no land to inherit drove many to seek their fortune abroad. Their boats loaded up with provisions, they set out across the Atlantic Ocean.

Viking ships set sail in search of adventure and new lands.

Time Line

A.D. 841
Norsemen establish a trading post in Ireland

A.D. 870
Settlement of Iceland

A.D. 986
Erik the Red founds settlement on Greenland

C. A.D. 1000
Leif Erikson sails to Vinland

C. A.D. 1010
Thorfinn Karlsefni fails to settle in Vinland

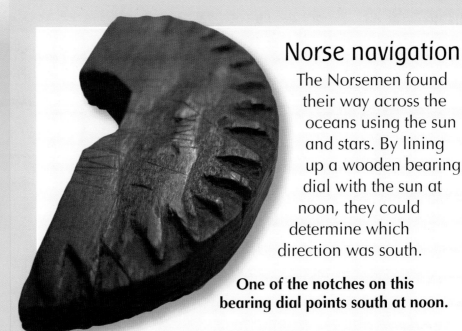

Norse navigation

The Norsemen found their way across the oceans using the sun and stars. By lining up a wooden bearing dial with the sun at noon, they could determine which direction was south.

One of the notches on this bearing dial points south at noon.

What Next?

By the 1400s, the climate of Greenland had become much colder, so the Vikings abandoned their settlements, leaving the island to its original Inuit inhabitants.

New world

The first Norse settlements were established in Ireland, the isles of Scotland, and the Faeroe Islands. By A.D. 870, the Norsemen had settled in Iceland. A century later, Erik the Red ventured across to Greenland, then much warmer than it is today. In A.D. 1000, the Norse leader Leif Erikson reached as far as Newfoundland, in Canada, and possibly further. A later attempt to settle the region by Thorfinn Karlsefni was unsuccessful and the Norsemen soon forgot about this new world.

Settling the new land

In 1960, a Norwegian archeologist, Helge Ingstad, discovered the foundation posts of two Norse houses at L'Anse aux Meadows, on the northern tip of Newfoundland, Canada. These houses may be the Vinland settlement, although some historians think Vinland was further down the coast, perhaps near Cape Cod.

A reconstruction of the Norse settlement at L'Anse aux Meadows.

A Viking voyage

The Vikings, or Norsemen, who sailed west from Norway across the North Atlantic Ocean were skilled and brave seafarers, risking their lives in open boats to search for new lands. Most could not read or write, so they passed on their stories by word of mouth. Many of these stories were later written down in the great Norse sagas. This is a fictional diary of a voyage along the main route to Greenland.

Due West

With great sadness I left my home in Bergen seven days ago bound for Greenland. We first sailed north some 30 miles until we made the Stad, a headland to our east. From there we headed straight out to sea. We have been told to sail a direct course west to Hvarf in Greenland. We are to sail north of Shetland, so that we will sight land only in clear weather, south of the Faeroes, then south of Iceland so that we can see the birds and whales from there.

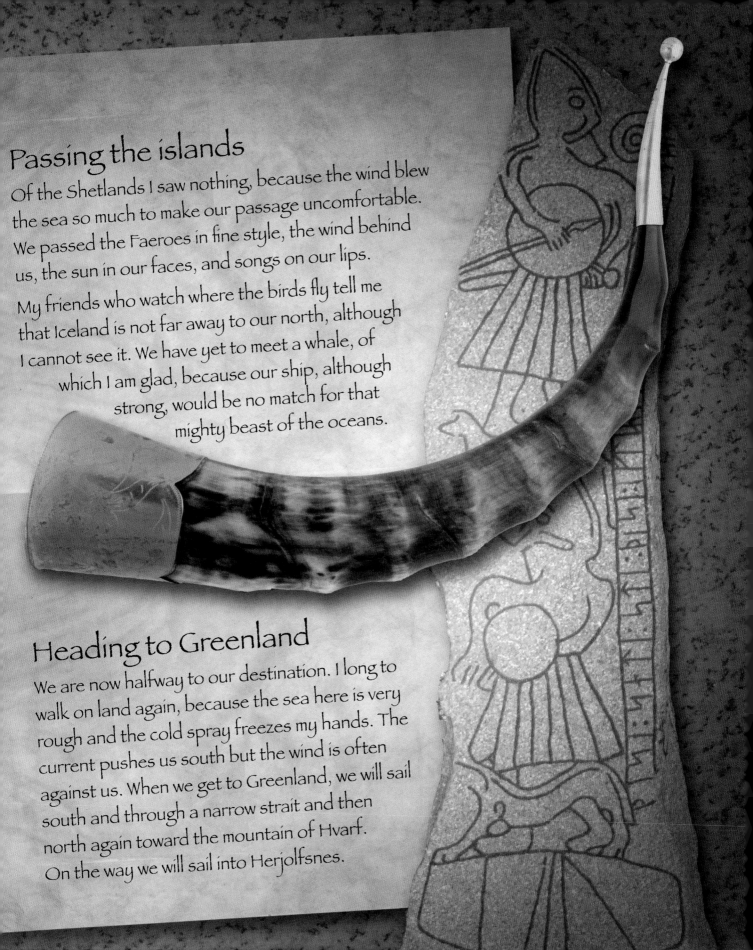

Passing the islands

Of the Shetlands I saw nothing, because the wind blew the sea so much to make our passage uncomfortable. We passed the Faeroes in fine style, the wind behind us, the sun in our faces, and songs on our lips.

My friends who watch where the birds fly tell me that Iceland is not far away to our north, although I cannot see it. We have yet to meet a whale, of which I am glad, because our ship, although strong, would be no match for that mighty beast of the oceans.

Heading to Greenland

We are now halfway to our destination. I long to walk on land again, because the sea here is very rough and the cold spray freezes my hands. The current pushes us south but the wind is often against us. When we get to Greenland, we will sail south and through a narrow strait and then north again toward the mountain of Hvarf. On the way we will sail into Herjolfsnes.

Journey to Mecca

At least once in their lives, Muslims try to make the hajj, or pilgrimage, to the sacred city of Mecca in Arabia. Getting there is straightforward today, but in the 1300s, this was the journey of a lifetime.

The long way around

In 1325, Ibn Battuta set off from Tangier, Morocco, to visit the holy cities of Islam. He traveled along the North African coast to Cairo and sailed up the Nile, hoping to cross overland to the Red Sea and on to Mecca. When this failed, he returned to Cairo and trekked through Palestine and Syria before reaching Mecca in 1327.

Ibn Battuta

In 1304, Ibn Battuta was born into a wealthy family of Muslim judges, so he was well educated. By the time of his death, in 1369, he had visited as many as 44 countries and traveled more than 71,500 miles (115,000 km).

Ancient wonder

Among the many amazing sights Ibn Battuta saw were the ruins of the Pharos lighthouse in Alexandria. One of the seven wonders of the ancient world, the lighthouse was built around 280 B.C. to guard the entrance to Alexandria.

The Pharos lighthouse, as it must once have looked.

It's Amazing!

Ibn Battuta wrote a chronicle of his journeys. Sometimes he exaggerated. He claimed he saw 12,000 bishops in a cathedral in Constantinople!

Sailing south

After his hajj, Ibn Battuta decided he would visit every Muslim country in the world. He crossed the Arabian desert to Iraq and Persia before returning to Mecca, where he studied law and religion. In 1330, he traveled down the Red Sea to the coast of East Africa.

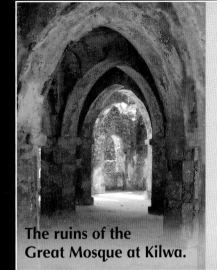

The ruins of the Great Mosque at Kilwa.

East Africa

In 1330, Ibn Battuta set out for East Africa. He visited the trading ports of Mombasa in Kenya and Kilwa in Tanzania, which he described as "one of the most beautiful and well-built of all cities." Many of the houses were built of coral and stone.

The Great Mosque in Mecca, the end point of the hajj.

Time Line

1304
Ibn Battuta born in Tangier

1325
Sets out for Cairo, and then sails up the Nile

1326
Visits Jerusalem, Damascus, and Syria

1327
Reaches Mecca, travels to Persia and Iraq

1328
Returns to Mecca

1330
Travels to East Africa, sailing as far as Kilwa

25

To the far east

In 1331, Ibn Battuta decided to seek employment with the Sultan of Delhi, in India. Needing a guide and translator, he went to Anatolia (Turkey) to join up with traders who traveled the Silk Road into Asia.

To India and beyond

Ibn Battuta first crossed the Black Sea to Russia. He then recrossed it in a large loop, via Constantinople, to central Asia, and on through Afghanistan to India. The sultan first employed Battuta as a judge, then offered him the post of ambassador to the Chinese emperor. Yet again, he was off on his travels. He sailed on a series of Chinese trading junks from southern India to the Chinese mainland via southeast Asia and Vietnam.

Ibn Fadlan

Ibn Battuta was not the first great Muslim traveler. In A.D. 921, Ibn Fadlan was sent by the Caliph of Baghdad to visit the King of the Bulgars of the Volga. He met the Rus Vikings of Russia, and was amazed by their tattoos.

It's Amazing!

Ibn Battuta was not impressed by everywhere he visited: "I did not like the land of China . . . I was troubled by their worship of statues."

The Maldives are lush tropical islands.

A break in the Maldives

On his journey from India to China, Ibn Battuta spent nine months in the Maldives in the Indian Ocean. The islands had converted from Buddhism to Islam, so he found employment as an Islamic judge. But his strict judgments were disliked among the happy-go-lucky Maldivians.

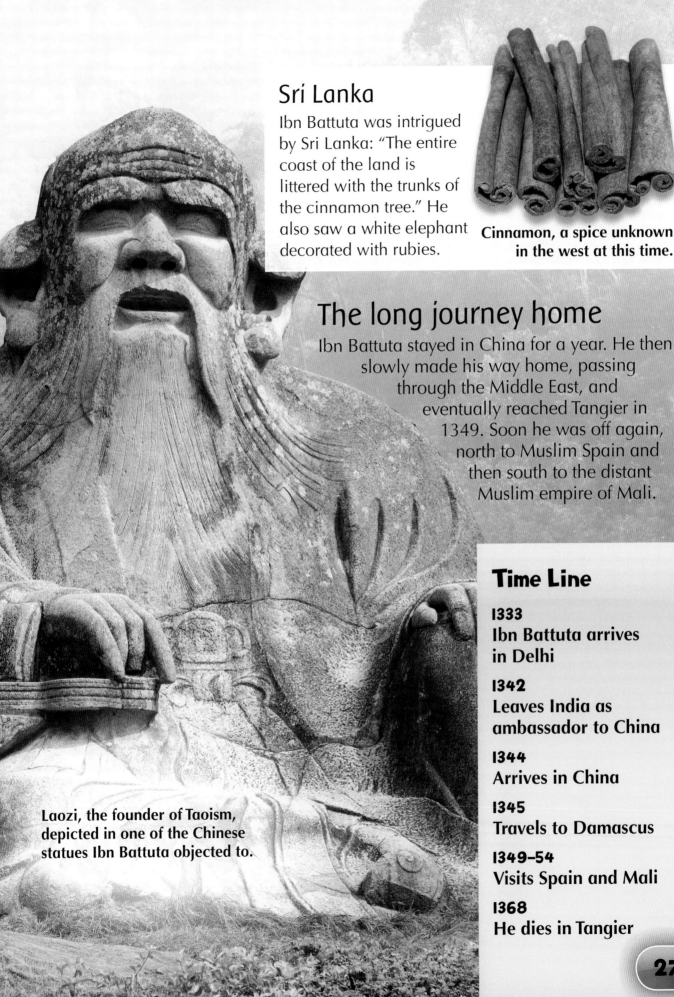

Sri Lanka

Ibn Battuta was intrigued by Sri Lanka: "The entire coast of the land is littered with the trunks of the cinnamon tree." He also saw a white elephant decorated with rubies.

Cinnamon, a spice unknown in the west at this time.

The long journey home

Ibn Battuta stayed in China for a year. He then slowly made his way home, passing through the Middle East, and eventually reached Tangier in 1349. Soon he was off again, north to Muslim Spain and then south to the distant Muslim empire of Mali.

Laozi, the founder of Taoism, depicted in one of the Chinese statues Ibn Battuta objected to.

Time Line

1333
Ibn Battuta arrives in Delhi

1342
Leaves India as ambassador to China

1344
Arrives in China

1345
Travels to Damascus

1349–54
Visits Spain and Mali

1368
He dies in Tangier

Missions to the Mongols

In 1241, the Mongol armies threatened Europe. Only the death of their ruler, the Great Khan Ogedai, made their soldiers turn back. The pope decided to make contact with the Mongols. Two Franciscan monks were sent on separate missions.

William acted on behalf of French King Louis IX.

Giovanni da Pian del Carpine

The 65-year-old Giovanni and a group of monks left Lyons in France in 1245. They headed east through central Europe and Russia until they met a Mongol patrol, not far from Kiev. They reached the capital of Karakorum in June 1246. Küyük, the new Mongol leader, sent them back with the message that unless the pope recognized his authority, "we will consider you our enemies." Giovanni had failed, but he had learned much about the Mongols.

William of Rubruck

William of Rubruck (c.1215–95) was a Flemish Franciscan monk with a good command of foreign languages. This made him an ideal ambassador to visit the Mongols.

Gengis Khan flanked by his two sons.

The Mongol Empire

By 1206, Genghis Khan had united the various Mongol tribes. He then set out on a campaign of conquest that took the Mongol armies into the center of Europe and south into China, Persia, and the Middle East. After 1241, the empire broke up into smaller "khanates." By the end of the century, it had collapsed.

What Next?

The journeys of Giovanni and William opened up the road from Europe into Asia. Merchants, such as the Polo family, benefited from their journeys.

A second mission

In 1253, a second monk, William of Rubruck, left Constantinople, this time purely as a missionary. He traveled to Karakorum to meet the new khan, Möngke. William was an observant traveler, the first to realize, for example, that the Caspian Sea was landlocked. He failed to convert the Mongols, but his mission did open the way for better relations between Christian west and Mongol east.

Even today, the Mongols are skilled archers, and both men and women compete in contests.

The Mongols

The Mongols were a group of nomadic tribes from the grassy steppes north of China. Their powerful armies were highly mobile and very disciplined, which allowed them to overwhelm their enemies.

Mongol horsemen were feared for their bravery and stamina.

Time Line

1206
Mongols unite under Genghis Khan

1241
Mongol armies rampage around central Europe

1245–46
Giovanni da Pian del Carpine visits the Great Khan Küyük

1253–55
William of Rubruck visits the Great Khan Möngke

1300
Mongol power is in decline; most Mongols have converted to Islam

To China and back

At a time when people rarely ventured out of their home town or village, and very few ever left their own country to travel abroad, the exploits of the Polo family in the 1200s were quite remarkable.

Time Line

1254
Marco Polo born in Venice

1259–69
Niccolo and Mafeo Polo make their first journey to China

1271–75
The Polos return to China with Marco

1295
The Polos arrive back in Venice

1298–99
Imprisoned by the Genoese, Marco Polo dictates *Il milione*, an account of his travels

1324
Marco Polo dies in Venice

Trading places

Niccolo and Mafeo Polo were merchants from Venice in Italy, who were keen to trade with the wealthy Mongol Empire of China. In 1259, they journeyed through Russia and central Asia as far as Khanbaliq (Beijing), the capital of the Mongol Empire. Here, they met the emperor, Kublai Khan. The two brothers returned to Venice in 1269.

The court of Kublai Khan

The Polos returned to China in 1271, this time with Niccolo's son, the 17-year-old Marco. They arrived at the summer palace of Kublai Khan (left) in Shang-du in May 1275.

Marco Polo

Marco Polo (1254–1324) was taken to China as a teenager. He worked for the Mongol emperor Kublai Khan for 20 years, becoming one of his most trusted servants. Polo spent much of this time traveling around China and Asia and learning about the region. In the 1290s, Marco returned to Venice with his father and uncle.

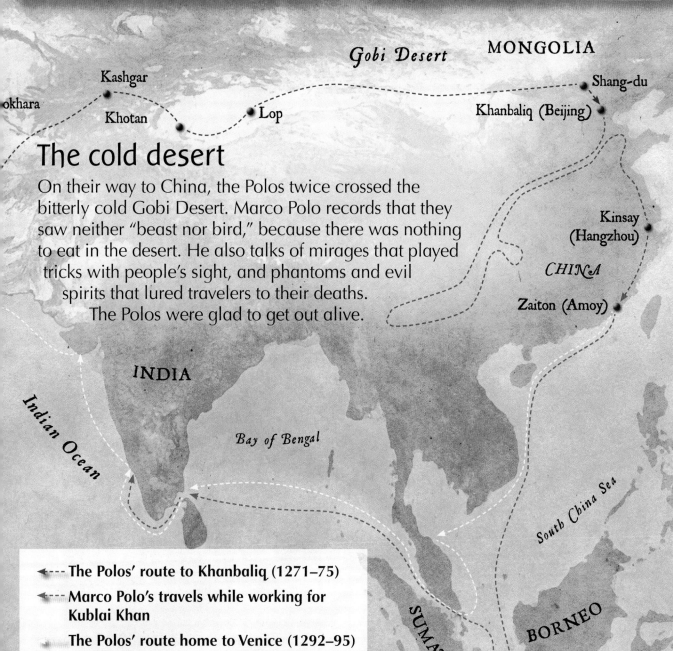

The cold desert

On their way to China, the Polos twice crossed the bitterly cold Gobi Desert. Marco Polo records that they saw neither "beast nor bird," because there was nothing to eat in the desert. He also talks of mirages that played tricks with people's sight, and phantoms and evil spirits that lured travelers to their deaths. The Polos were glad to get out alive.

Gobi Desert — MONGOLIA
Kashgar
okhara
Khotan
Lop
Shang-du
Khanbaliq (Beijing)
Kinsay (Hangzhou)
CHINA
Zaiton (Amoy)
INDIA
Indian Ocean
Bay of Bengal
South China Sea
SUMATRA
BORNEO
JAVA

◄--- The Polos' route to Khanbaliq (1271–75)

◄--- Marco Polo's travels while working for Kublai Khan

◄--- The Polos' route home to Venice (1292–95)

The seven voyages of Zheng He

In 1405, Emperor Yongle ruled over the Ming Empire in China. To show his neighbors just how powerful his empire was, Yongle sent a naval expedition to sail around the region, led by the court official Zheng He.

The imperial fleet

Zheng He commanded an impressive fleet of over 300 sea-going junks. The largest was 450 feet (140 m) long and had nine masts. More than 28,000 sailors were required to sail this vast fleet, which was designed to impress, not to conquer territory. When each region's ruler saw at first hand the power of the Ming Empire, he would happily acknowledge that Yongle was the most powerful emperor of all.

Emperor Yongle, Zhu Yuanzhang's son and the third emperor of the Ming Dynasty.

Time Line

1371
Zheng He born in Yunnan province

1402
Yongle becomes the third Ming emperor

1405–07
Zheng He's first voyage, to southeast Asia and India

1407–22
Zheng He makes five more voyages

1426
New emperor Xuande withdraws support from Zheng He

1433
Zheng He dies at sea during his seventh voyage

The Ming Dynasty

In 1356, the Chinese, led by a peasant and former Buddhist monk, Zhu Yuanzhang, rose up against their Mongol overlords. Zhu seized Beijing, the Mongol capital, in 1368. He declared himself Emperor Hongwu, first of the new Ming Dynasty. The Ming brought great wealth to China until they were overthrown by the Manchus in 1644.

China from China

In the mid-1300s, Chinese potters began to make pure, white porcelain decorated with bright cobalt blue. Zheng He gave porcelain to the kings he met on his travels. In return, he was given animals, such as zebras and giraffes, which he took back to the zoo in Beijing.

A late Ming Dynasty blue-and-white porcelain plate dating from the 16th century.

The Forbidden City in Beijing, built after Emperor Yongle made Beijing the Chinese capital in 1420.

The voyages

Zheng He made seven voyages between 1405 and 1433. His first three voyages took him around southeast Asia and on to India and Sri Lanka. On later voyages he reached as far west as Arabia and the east African coast. Everywhere he went, he handed out Chinese silks, porcelain, and other fine goods. In total, Zheng He visited more than 30 kingdoms. He died on a voyage around the Indian Ocean.

It's Amazing!

The records of Zheng He's last two voyages were destroyed. He may have visited the west coast of America and New Zealand.

Pointing the way

Around A.D. 1100, the Chinese discovered that a magnetized needle always points in the same direction. They used this discovery to make a compass to help sailors find their way on their voyages.

A Chinese box compass.

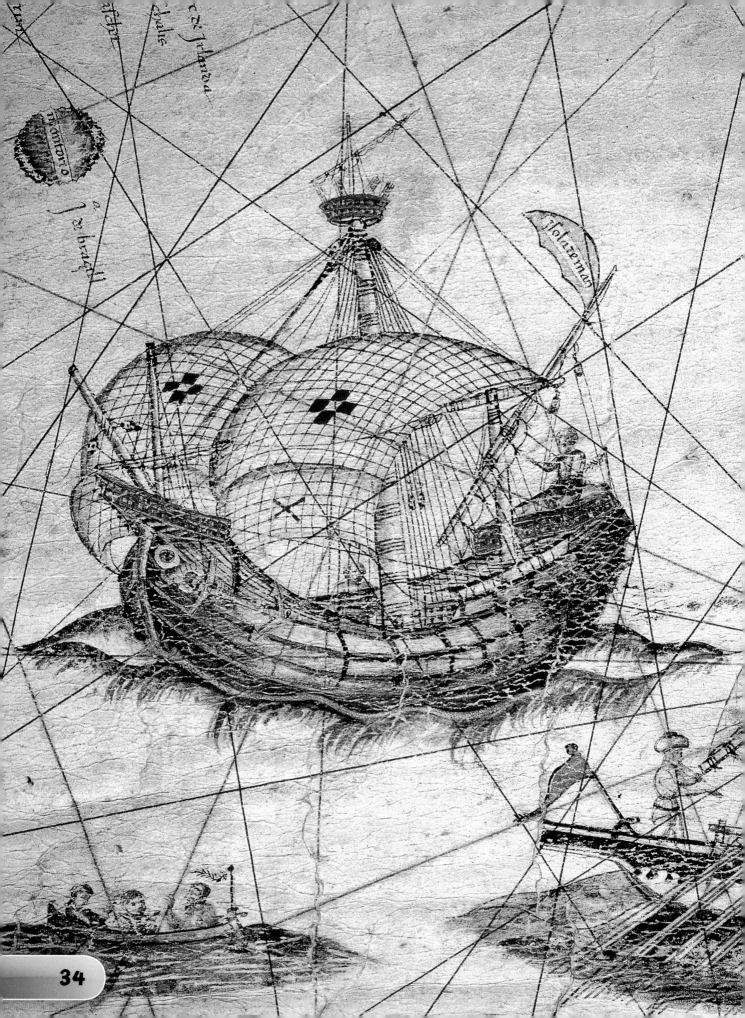

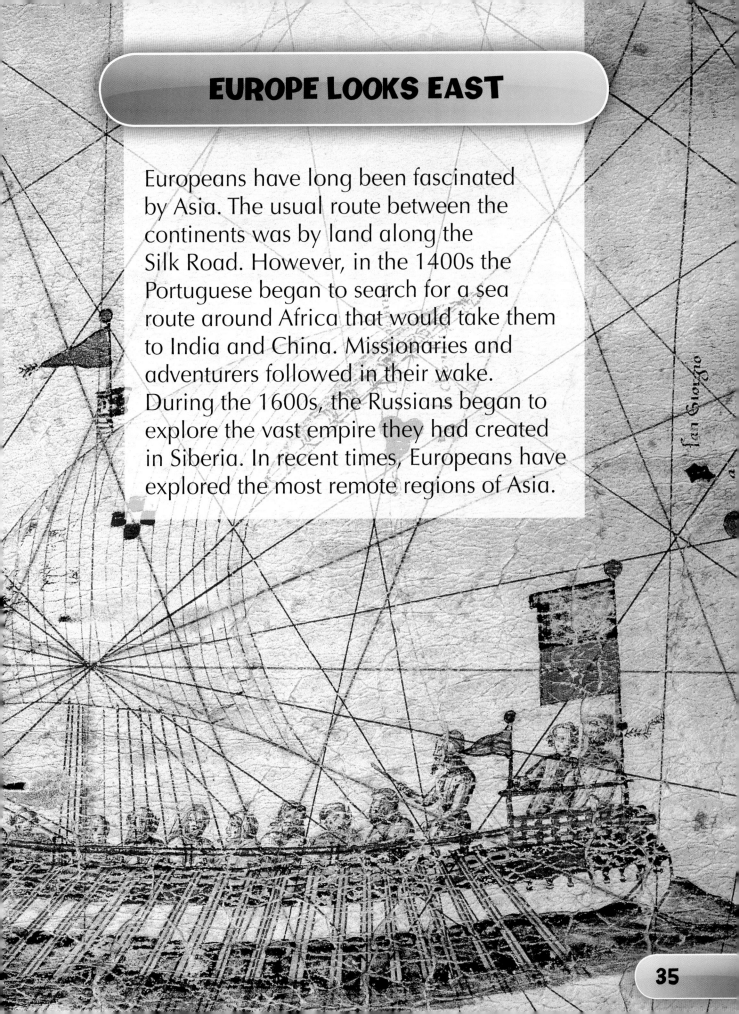

EUROPE LOOKS EAST

Europeans have long been fascinated by Asia. The usual route between the continents was by land along the Silk Road. However, in the 1400s the Portuguese began to search for a sea route around Africa that would take them to India and China. Missionaries and adventurers followed in their wake. During the 1600s, the Russians began to explore the vast empire they had created in Siberia. In recent times, Europeans have explored the most remote regions of Asia.

Prince Henry the Navigator

Henry the Navigator was a 15th-century Portuguese prince. Although he did no exploring himself, it could be said that he did more for exploration than anyone before or since.

An interest in Africa

In 1415, the Portuguese seized the city of Ceuta in Morocco from its Muslim rulers. Among the victorious army was Prince Henrique (Henry), son of King João I. The campaign inspired Henry to learn more about Africa. With his father's support, he set up a school of navigation at Sagres in southwest Portugal. From here, fleets of ships set out to explore the west African coastline.

Prince Henry

Prince Henry (1394–1460) used his personal wealth to sponsor voyages, and encouraged Portuguese sailors to investigate the lands and oceans to their south.

The navigation school

Founded in 1418, the navigation school at Sagres taught mapmaking, geography, and astronomy, all essential tools for any explorer. Armed with these skills, Portuguese captains and pilots were able to map new lands so that future expeditions could benefit from their experience.

A Portuguese map from 1485, showing the west coasts of Europe and Africa.

New route to Asia

In 1453, the Portuguese voyages assumed a new urgency. The Muslim Ottoman Turks had taken the city of Constantinople and totally blocked the Silk Road from Europe to Asia. The Portuguese needed to discover a sea route around Africa that would take them to the wealth of India and China.

A drawing of a caravel from the 15th century.

The caravel

The Portuguese developed a new type of ship known as the caravel. Narrower than its predecessors, the caravel was easy to maneuver and better able to withstand storms. It had a hold in which to store the supplies necessary for a long voyage.

What Next?

The navigational skills and better ships developed by the Portuguese ultimately allowed European nations to dominate the world's seas, and the lands around them.

A contemporary picture of the Portuguese capital, Lisbon.

Time Line

1415
Portuguese capture Ceuta in Africa

1418
Prince Henry founds navigation school

1427
Portuguese sailors begin exploring the west African coast

1444
Portuguese reach the Senegal River

1471
Trading post at Elmina in Ghana is established

1472
Lopo Gonçalves is first European to cross the equator

Edging down the coast

By 1480, the Portuguese had crossed the equator and begun to map the coastline of southern Africa. They still did not know if they would find a sea route to India and the east, because the African coast seemed to go on forever.

Diogo Cão

The voyages of Diogo Cão (c.1450–86), a Portuguese explorer, did much to open up the sea route to India. His mapping of the Congo River helped many future navigators in the region.

Cão's first voyage

In 1482, Diogo Cão set off from the capital, Lisbon. He sailed down the North African coast and stopped for supplies at the fort of Elmina in Ghana. He then turned south. When Cão reached the mouth of the Congo River, he erected a stone padrão, or pillar, on its southern bank. He sailed upstream, hoping it would lead him around Africa, before turning back.

The fort of Elmina in Ghana was used by the Portuguese for trade, including the slave trade.

1482
Diogo Cão sails south to the Congo River via Elmina in Ghana. Sails as far as Cape Santa Maria in Angola before returning home

1484
Arrives back in Lisbon and is knighted by the king for his efforts

1484–85
Cão returns to the Congo River and sails upstream before rapids force him to turn back

1486
Sails south to Cape Cross where he dies

Sand dunes on the Namib coastline.

Namibia

Diogo Cão sailed down the coast of Namibia but found it to be a hot desert with no natural harbors. He died somewhere off Cape Cross, a few miles away from Walvis Bay, one of the finest natural harbors on the entire coast.

Pushing south

In 1482, Cão sailed south to Cape Santa Maria in Angola, where he erected a padrão before returning to Lisbon. In 1484, he set off again, this time sailing right up the Congo before rapids closed his route. He then headed even farther south, erecting a padrão at Cape Cross in Namibia. At this point, his life ended, either shipwrecked on Cape Cross or lost at sea.

It's Amazing!

King João II sponsored Cão's second voyage in 1484 rather than support a voyage across the Atlantic proposed by Christopher Columbus.

The padrão

King João gave Diogo Cão 5-foot (1.5-m)-high limestone padrãos, or pillars, each topped with a cross and inscribed with the names of the king and the expedition commander. Cão placed the pillars in significant places to guide future explorers.

A limestone padrão with the Portuguese royal coat of arms carved on it.

Reaching the Indian Ocean

By 1487, the Portuguese had mapped most of the west African coastline, but there appeared to be no route around it to India. One man, Bartolomeu Dias, proved this to be wrong.

The end of Africa

In 1487, Dias sailed out of Lisbon with two caravels and one supply ship. By the end of the year, he had made it south of Cape Cross. After passing the Orange River, a huge storm blew up that forced him in a southerly direction for 13 days. When it calmed, he headed east, expecting land. Instead, he found more sea.

EUROPE

Lisbon

- - - - → outbound journey
← - - - - inbound journey

Cape Verde

Elmina

AFRICA

Atlantic Ocean

Congo River

Cape Cross

Orange River

Great Fish River

Cape of Good Hope

Mossel Bay

Algoa Bay

The Cape of Good Hope on the southwest tip of Africa.

Cape of Good Hope

As Dias sailed west on his voyage home, he caught his first sight of the Cape of Good Hope. The name was suggested by Dias, although some historians credit King João with naming it.

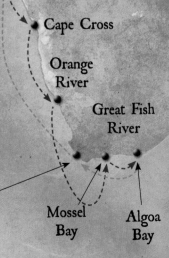

Bartolomeu Dias

Bartolomeu Dias (c.1450–1500) added some 1,250 miles (2,016 km) to the length of African coastline known to Europeans. After his own successful voyage, he accompanied Vasco da Gama on the first leg of his voyage to India in 1497. He was one of the commanders in Pedro Cabral's fleet that discovered Brazil in 1500. He died later in the same expedition.

It's Amazing!

Dias was the first navigator to take a spare ship filled with supplies. He left it off the west African coast, but returned to find that the provisions had been looted.

Into the Indian Ocean

Dias turned north, landing at present-day Mossel Bay, 200 miles (320 km) east of the Cape of Good Hope. He then sailed farther east to Algoa Bay and then on to a river he named the Rio de Infante, probably the one known today as the Great Fish River, where he erected a padrão. By now Dias was in the Indian Ocean, having rounded the southern tip of Africa. When his crew forced him to return, he sailed back west along the coast, sighting the Cape of Good Hope before he turned north to Elmina.

Indian Ocean

Time Line

1487
Dias sets sail from Lisbon with a fleet of three ships

1488
Dias is blown south by a storm and sails past the Cape of Good Hope into the Southern Ocean

1488
Dias enters Indian Ocean

1497
Dias sails with Vasco da Gama

1500
Dias sails with Cabral, discovering Brazil, then dies in a storm

The route to India

Now that Bartolomeu Dias had discovered a route around Africa into the Indian Ocean, the sea route was open to India and the east. The man to open up that route was Vasco da Gama.

Around the Cape

Da Gama set sail from Lisbon in July 1497. He stopped in the Cape Verde Islands for a week in July and then headed south into the Atlantic, away from the unpredictable winds and tides along the African coast. After 96 days he made landfall in St. Helena Bay on the west coast of South Africa. From there he edged around the Cape of Good Hope into the Indian Ocean and up the east coast of Africa to Mombasa and Malindi in Kenya.

Vasco da Gama

Vasco da Gama (c.1460–1524) was a ruthless Portuguese sailor whose voyage to India in 1497 opened up a new sea route to the east. Honored by King Manuel I as Admiral of India, da Gama returned in 1502 to win control over the spice trade.

A Portuguese map of India from the 16th century.

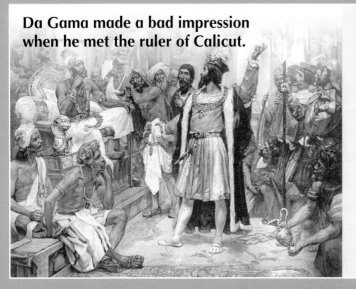

Da Gama made a bad impression when he met the ruler of Calicut.

In Calicut

Once in India, da Gama met the Hindu ruler of Calicut, but the gifts he offered him were of poor quality. The Muslims who controlled the spice trade in the region feared Portuguese intentions, and tried to get the local Hindus to destroy their fleet. Da Gama was lucky to get away.

Navigation tools

Early navigators used an astrolabe or a quadrant to work out latitude—how far north or south the ship was. The astrolabe measured the height of the sun, the quadrant the height of a star. It was not possible to measure longitude—how far east or west—accurately until the mid-18th century.

An early astrolabe, used to calculate latitude.

To India and back

Da Gama headed northeast from Malindi across the Indian Ocean. The favorable winds took him straight to Calicut in southern India, where he made landfall in May 1498. His mission accomplished, he set off home in August. His return was much harder because of unfavorable winds in the Indian Ocean, and he did not reach Lisbon until September 1499.

Time Line

1497
Da Gama leaves Lisbon with four ships

1498
Sails up the east African coast and across the Indian Ocean to Calicut

1499
Reaches Lisbon with one ship and one fourth of his crew still alive

1502–3
Returns to India and ruthlessly enforces Portuguese control over the spice trade

1524
Da Gama dies in India

It's Amazing!
Da Gama's expedition led to the establishment of colonies in India, which remained in Portuguese hands until 1961.

A Portuguese sailor

Prince Henry the Navigator sponsored many voyages to explore the coastline of Africa. One set sail in 1456 under the Venetian Alvise da Cadamosto (1432–c.1480). They sailed up the Gambia River, noting the mighty baobab tree and the hippo. Here we imagine the diary of a member of the crew.

The voyage south

I sail onboard a caravel under the captaincy of Alvise da Cadamosto, a man from the port of Venice, although I myself come from our capital, Lisbon. We sail south to explore the coastline of Africa so that our knowledge of it might lead to good trade, or perhaps to convert its heathen people to the way of our Lord.

Cape Verde Islands

After we left the islands of the Canaries, we sailed past Cape Branco and into the open sea. I have not sailed without sight of land before and feared for my safety. God be praised, no harm came to us and we made our passage safely.

A mighty storm raged for three days and blew us off our course. When the storm calmed we saw two islands that we later found were empty of people. We have named these islands Boavista and Santiago and claimed them for our king.

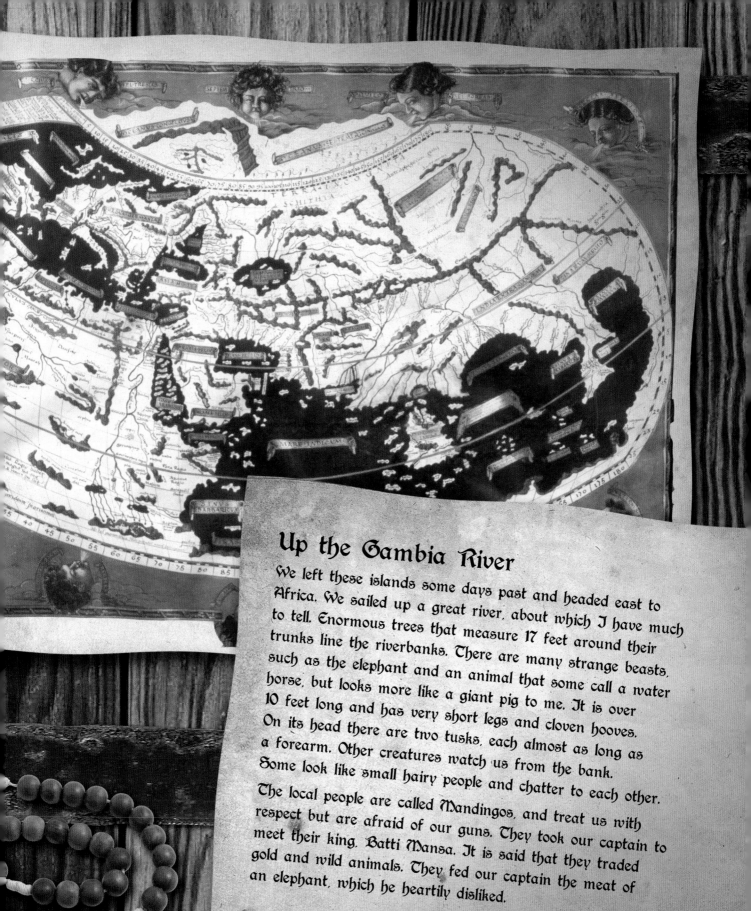

Up the Gambia River

We left these islands some days past and headed east to Africa. We sailed up a great river, about which I have much to tell. Enormous trees that measure 17 feet around their trunks line the riverbanks. There are many strange beasts, such as the elephant and an animal that some call a water horse, but looks more like a giant pig to me. It is over 10 feet long and has very short legs and cloven hooves. On its head there are two tusks, each almost as long as a forearm. Other creatures watch us from the bank. Some look like small hairy people and chatter to each other.

The local people are called Mandingos, and treat us with respect but are afraid of our guns. They took our captain to meet their king, Batti Mansa. It is said that they traded gold and wild animals. They fed our captain the meat of an elephant, which he heartily disliked.

Travelers and missionaries

The voyages of early navigators opened up the coastline of Asia to European traders. But it was not until the mid-1500s that European missionaries began to explore inland.

Missionary zeal

The Jesuit order was determined to convert Asia to Christianity. Spanish priest Francis Xavier was the first to go. He was followed by the Portuguese Bento de Goes (1562–1607), who from 1602 to 1607 traveled through central Asia into China in search of a lost Christian community.

The body of Saint Francis Xavier on display in Goa, India.

Saint Francis Xavier

The son of a Basque nobleman, Francis Xavier (1506–52) was a founder member of the Jesuits. He spent several years in India and Sri Lanka before sailing for Japan, where he arrived in 1549. He was made a saint after baptizing the most people since St. Paul.

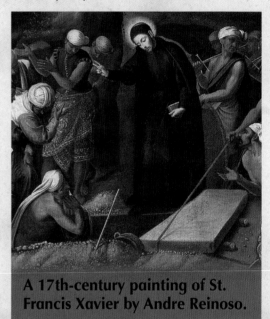

A 17th-century painting of St. Francis Xavier by Andre Reinoso.

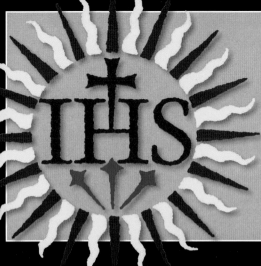

The Jesuits

The Society of Jesus, also called the Jesuits, is a Roman Catholic religious order. It was founded by Ignatius Loyola and six other trainee priests in 1534, originally to convert Muslims to Christianity. It soon widened its activities to cover India and China.

The seal of the Society of Jesus.

It's Amazing!

St. Francis Xavier died off the coast of China. His body was brought to Goa, but his right forearm, which he used to baptize converts, was removed and taken to Rome.

The forbidden city

Two Jesuits, German John Grueber (1623–80) and Belgian Albert d'Orville (1621–62) set out in 1661 to find a land route between China and India to avoid Dutch raiders on the China Sea. They crossed the Himalayas, becoming the first Europeans to visit the sacred city of Lhasa in Tibet.

A Tibetan yak, well adapted for life on the "roof of the world."

A strange continent

European knowledge of Asia was still extremely vague in the 1600s. Grueber and d'Orville were amazed when, traveling into Tibet, they exchanged their horses for strange beasts of burden called yaks.

Time Line

1541–52
Francis Xavier visits India, Sri Lanka, China, and Japan to convert people to Christianity

1602–7
Bento de Goes seeks lost Christian community said to exist between China and India

1624–26
Antonio de Andrade becomes first European to cross the Himalayas

1661
Grueber and d'Orville travel from China through Tibet to India

Into Siberia

During the 1600s, the Russian Empire expanded eastward across Siberia to the Pacific Ocean. The Russian czar Peter the Great knew little about his new realm, and decided to find out more.

Heading east

In 1724, Peter appointed Vitus Bering to lead an expedition of discovery to Siberia. His task was to travel overland to the Pacific coastline of the Kamchatka peninsula in eastern Siberia. He was then to sail north to discover whether Siberia and Asia were connected to North America.

Asia

North America

The Bering Strait, which separates Asia from North America, as seen from space.

Vitus Bering

Vitus Bering (1681–1741) was born in Denmark, and became one of the hundreds of western Europeans recruited by Peter the Great to modernize his backward country. Bering was a superb organizer, and twice arranged large-scale expeditions to one of the most remote places on the Earth.

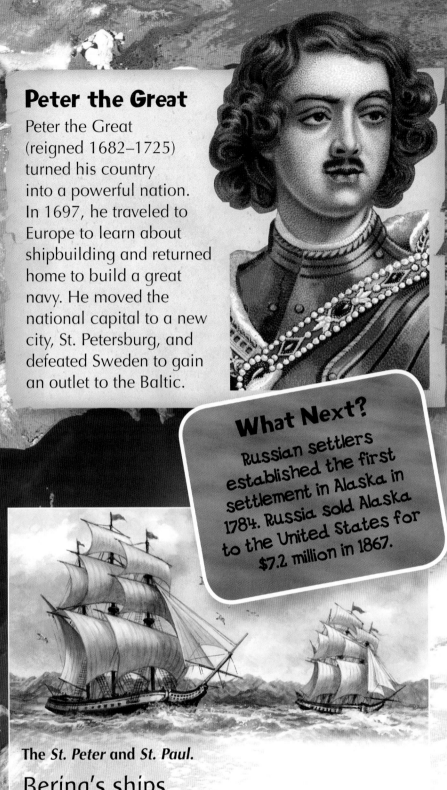

Peter the Great

Peter the Great (reigned 1682–1725) turned his country into a powerful nation. In 1697, he traveled to Europe to learn about shipbuilding and returned home to build a great navy. He moved the national capital to a new city, St. Petersburg, and defeated Sweden to gain an outlet to the Baltic.

What Next?

Russian settlers established the first settlement in Alaska in 1784. Russia sold Alaska to the United States for $7.2 million in 1867.

The *St. Peter* and *St. Paul*.

Bering's ships

Bering was a skilled shipbuilder. He twice built small ships to sail from Okhotsk to Kamchatka. He then built three sea-going ships to explore the strait between Asia and North America: the *St. Gabriel* on his first expedition, the *St. Peter* and *St. Paul* on his second.

Time Line

1724
Vitus Bering commands an expedition to Siberia

1727
Bering and his team arrive in Okhotsk on the Siberian coast

1728
After crossing Kamchatka, he sets sail north, turning south a month later

1729
Bering retraces his steps across Siberia

1730
Back in St. Petersburg, Bering fails to convince everyone that he completed the task

Qualified success

In 1728, Bering sailed northward up the Pacific coast of Siberia into the strait that separates Siberia from Alaska and now bears his name. Fog prevented him from seeing land, but Bering was convinced that the two continents were not joined. Back in St. Petersburg, however, the authorities were not convinced, and ordered Bering to go back.

Mapping the North

In 1733, Vitus Bering set off once more for Siberia, this time in charge of one of the most ambitious explorations ever organized. The Great Northern Expedition aimed to map the entire coastline of Siberia, as well as many of the region's great rivers.

The death of Bering

It took Bering eight years to travel beyond Siberia. He finally set sail from Kamchatka to Alaska in June 1741. He sailed to the south Alaskan coast but, sick and short of food, he was forced to make his way back via the Aleutian Islands. In November 1741, Bering and his crew were shipwrecked on the island that is now named after him. Bering died, but his crew survived and sailed home the following year.

Alexei Chirikov

Captain Alexei Chirikov (1703–48) was Bering's second in command. Chirikov lost contact with Bering off Alaska but he managed to get his ship and crew back to Siberia, although many lost their lives to scurvy and hostile Inuits in Alaska.

Vitus Bering died while he and his crew were iced in on the island that is now named after him.

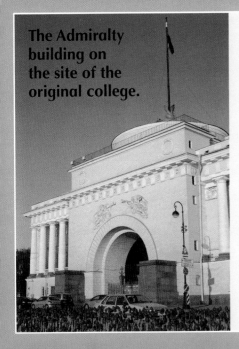

The Admiralty building on the site of the original college.

Imperial Admiralty College

The Great Northern Expedition was organized by the Imperial Admiralty College in St. Petersburg. Vitus Bering was given the task of traveling to the Pacific, while groups of naval officers divided the exploration of the north coast of Siberia and its rivers between them.

Exploring Siberia

The rest of the expedition had much more success. The great Ob, Yenisei, and Lena rivers that flow north into the Arctic Ocean were all explored. So was the Arctic coast from Archangel in the west to the Kolyma River in the far east of Siberia. The teams had plenty of manpower, but there was little backup and fewer supplies. They were often not heard of for years at a time.

Wolf carcasses hang up waiting to be skinned.

Fur trappers

The expedition into Siberia opened the way for fur trappers and traders to exploit the animal wealth of the region. Mink, sable, bear, and other wild animals were all trapped for their valuable furs and skins.

Time Line

1733
The Great Northern Expedition sets off for Siberia

1735–41
Teams explore the Arctic coastline and Siberian rivers

1741
Bering and Chirikov set sail from Petropavlovsk in Kamchatka to southern Alaskan coast; Bering dies on the return journey

1742
Semion Chelyuskin discovers Cape Chelyuskin, the northernmost point of Siberia

It's Amazing!

After Bering died, his crew built a small boat out of the wreckage of their ship, the St. Peter, and used it to sail to safety.

Along the Silk Road

Although Europeans had learned much about Asia by the 19th century, the center of the continent between the Russian, Chinese, and British Indian empires was largely unknown. Tibet was still forbidden territory, while the old Silk Road had largely been forgotten.

The Cave of the Thousand Buddhas, visited by Aurel Stein in 1907.

Crossing the deserts

In 1890, the Swedish explorer Sven Hedin set out on the first of his four epic expeditions. During 45 years, he mapped large parts of central Asia, exploring the Silk Road and crossing the vast Taklimakan and Gobi deserts of western China and Mongolia. His only failure occurred in 1901, when he tried but failed to enter the forbidden holy city of Lhasa in Tibet.

Sven Hedin, center, holding one of his maps.

Sven Hedin

The Swedish explorer Sven Hedin (1865–1952) was a skilled linguist. He worked as a diplomat and interpreter for the Swedish government, which sponsored two of his expeditions. On his final expedition, from 1933 to 1935, he completed a detailed map of the old Silk Road for the Chinese government.

1890
Sven Hedin begins first of four expeditions

1899–1902
Hedin discovers the ancient city of Lou-lan in the Taklimakan Desert

1900–2
Aurel Stein explores the Taklimakan Desert

1906–8
Hedin finds the source of the Indus and Brahmaputra rivers

1907
Aurel Stein discovers the *Diamond Sutra*

1933–35
Hedin maps Silk Road

The Tilla-Kari Madrassa in Samarkand, visited by Stein in 1914.

The intrepid archeologist

Sir Marc Aurel Stein (1862–1943) was a Hungarian archeologist who became a British citizen. He led four major expeditions in central Asia after 1900, traveling more than 25,000 miles (40,000 km) and collecting ancient artifacts and manuscripts.

Collector or thief?

Inspired by Hedin, the British archeologist Sir Marc Aurel Stein explored the Chinese end of the Silk Road, looking for ancient documents to bring back to Great Britain for research. Although Stein's discoveries were really important, many people criticized his methods: the Chinese called him a "foreign devil," robbing them of their archeological heritage.

The *Diamond Sutra*

In 1907, Aurel Stein discovered 40,000 scrolls in the Cave of the Thousand Buddhas at Dunhuang in western China. Among them was the *Diamond Sutra*, the world's oldest known printed book, dating from A.D. 868.

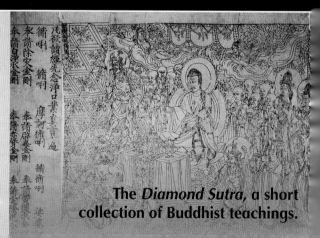

The *Diamond Sutra*, a short collection of Buddhist teachings.

Into Arabia

Among the parts of Asia least known to Europeans were the deserts of Syria and Arabia, and the two Muslim holy cities of Mecca and Medina, both closed to non-Muslims. During the 19th century, a number of Europeans visited this remote area and were amazed at what they found.

It's Amazing!

Petra is entered through a narrow gap in the rocks only 10 to 13 feet (3 to 4 m) wide. A monastery, church, tombs, and other buildings have been carved out of the solid red rock.

Forgotten city

Johann Ludwig Burckhardt arrived in Syria under the assumed name of Sheikh Ibrahim ibn Abdullah. In 1812, he headed south toward Egypt and visited Petra, a city carved into solid rock from the 2nd century B.C. He was the first Westerner in modern times to visit the forgotten city, which only became fully accessible to foreigners in the 1920s.

Petra, described by poet J. W. Burgon as the "rose-red city half as old as time."

Burckhardt, disguised as an Arab sheikh.

Johann Ludwig Burckhardt

Johann Ludwig Burckhardt (1784–1817) was born in Lausanne, Switzerland. When he moved to London in 1806, Burckhardt became intrigued by the idea of visiting foreign lands. He traveled first to Syria and then to Egypt and Arabia, before dying of dysentery in Cairo.

The holy cities

After some time in Egypt, a disguised Burckhardt crossed the Red Sea and visited Mecca and Medina. Explorers Richard Burton and Charles Doughty followed in his path, but Doughty was much more interested in the Bedouin who lived in the surrounding desert.

T. E. Lawrence, a great admirer of Doughty's book.

Arabia Deserta

The English explorer Charles Doughty lived for two years with the Bedouin of the Syrian and Arabian deserts. In 1888, he published his journal, *Travels in Arabia Deserta*. The book was little known until it was championed in the 1920s by famed scholar T. E. Lawrence.

Desert dwellers

The Bedouin are seminomadic tribespeople who live in the deserts of Syria and Arabia. They travel with their flocks in search of water and the occasional pasture. They live in tents and are immensely skilled at coping with the intense heat and lack of water.

A Bedouin encampment in the desert.

Time Line

1812
Johann Ludwig Burckhardt is the first Westerner to visit Petra

1814–15
Burckhardt visits Mecca and Medina

1815–16
Burckhardt visits the ancient monasteries on the Sinai Peninsula

1853
Richard Burton visits the holy cities dressed as an Afghan doctor

1876–78
Charles Doughty lives with the Bedouin of Arabia

The Empty Quarter

In the last century, most of the world was explored, its peoples visited, and its cultures described. Modern travelers have, therefore, sought out the most inaccessible areas, and the most distant and self-sufficient peoples.

Across the desert

The desert of southeast Saudi Arabia is known as the Rub' al Khali, the "Empty Quarter," because it has no roads and few people or animals. Bertram Thomas crossed the Rub' al Khali in 1930–31, the first European to do so. His book *Arabia Felix* (1932) describes the desert's people and their culture.

Bertram Thomas

In 1925, the British civil servant Bertram Thomas (1892–1950) became finance minister to the Sultan of Oman. As part of his duties, he made several expeditions into the desert.

Bedouin men from around the time Thomas traveled with them.

Time Line

1925–32
Bertram Thomas is finance minister to the Sultan of Oman

1930–31
Thomas crosses the Empty Quarter

1945–49
Wilfred Thesiger travels around the Empty Quarter, maps the Liwa oasis and the Umm As-Sammim quicksands

1951–58
Thesiger lives with the Marsh Arabs of Iraq

Wilfred Thesiger traveling with the Bedouin in the Arabian Desert.

Wilfred Thesiger

The son of a British diplomat, Wilfred Thesiger (1910–2003) was born in Addis Ababa, capital of Ethiopia. He traveled all his life and, in the 1930s, he was the first European to visit parts of northern Ethiopia. Later, he traveled extensively around Saudi Arabia, Iraq, and Kenya.

Thesiger took thousands of photographs using a Leica 2 similar to this one.

The wanderer

By his own words, Wilfred Thesiger had a "strange compulsion" to wander the deserts of the world, living as the people of the area lived. His travels took him to Africa, the mountains of central Asia, and the deserts of Arabia. Between 1945–49, Thesiger explored the entire Empty Quarter. He particularly admired the Bedouin way of life.

Reed boats, such as this one, are the Marsh Arabs' main form of transport.

The Marsh Arabs

The Marsh Arabs are the inhabitants of the marsh islands in southern Iraq. They live by raising water buffalo, growing crops, and weaving reeds. The area has always been isolated from the rest of Iraq and provided a shelter for escaped slaves.

What Next?

In the 1990s, Saddam Hussein, then dictator of Iraq, tried to drain the marshes and expel the Marsh Arabs. Today, only a few thousand of the original half a million inhabitants remain.

Intrepid women

Almost all explorers have been men, because women have traditionally lacked the independence to travel for themselves. However, during the early 20th century, two women became renowned explorers.

Caspian Sea

Elburz Mountains

◎ Alamut

◎ Tehran

◎ Mosul

P E R S I A

Euphrates River

◎ Kirkuk

I R A Q

Tigris River

Palmyra ◎

◎ Damascus

◎ Amman

Ar Ramadi ◎

◎ Baghdad

P A L E S T I N E

T R A N S - J O R D A N

◎ An Najaf

◎ Al Jawf

Mediterranean Sea

S E B E L   S H A M M A R

Kuwait ◎

◎ Hail

Persian Gulf

- - - ▶ Gertrude Bell's journey to central Arabia 1913–14

◎ Places visited by Freya Stark while based in Baghdad 1928–32

◎ Towns on Gertrude Bell's route

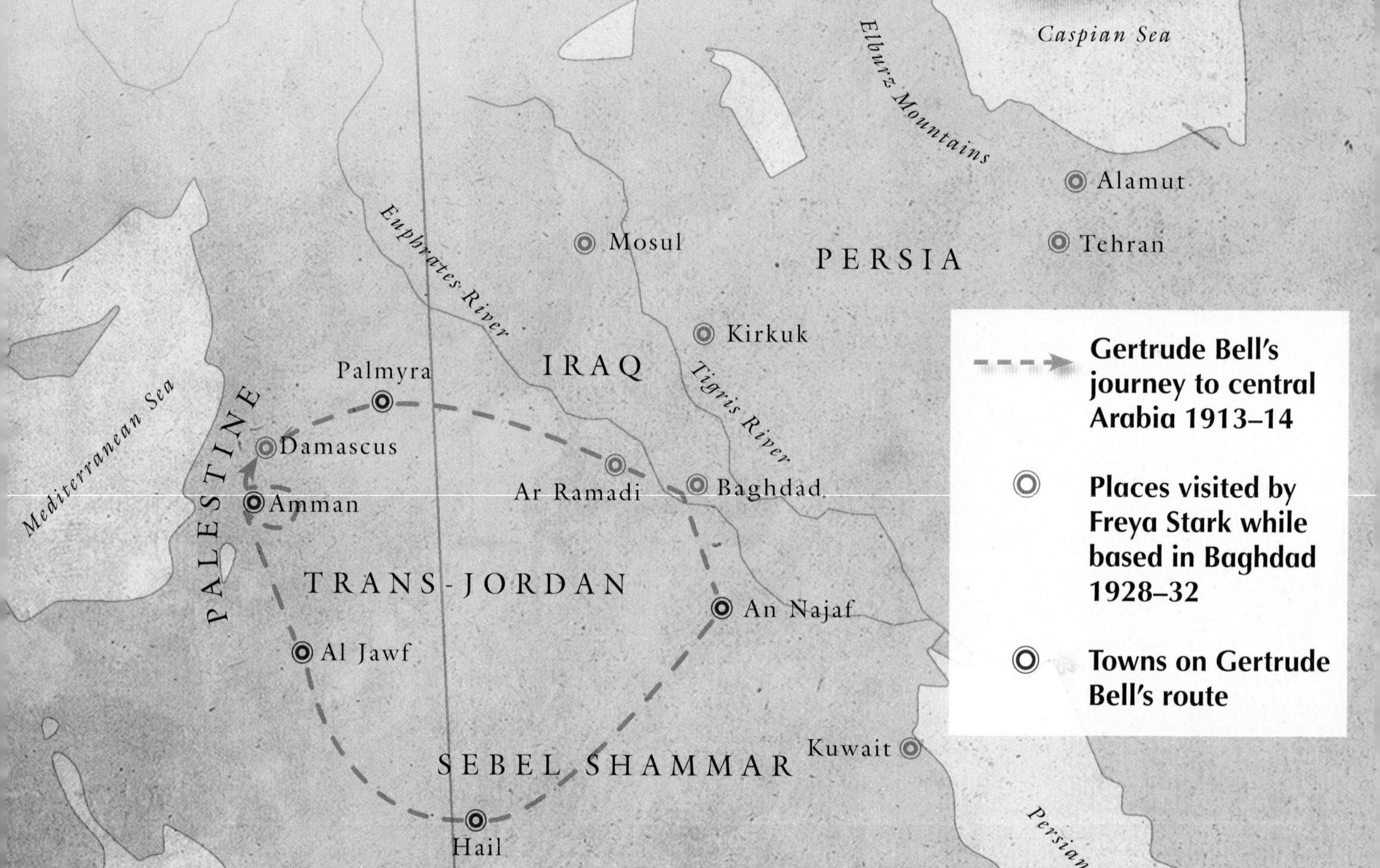

Setting the border

In 1905, British archeologist Gertrude Bell first explored the Syrian Desert. She almost lost her life on another expedition into central Arabia in 1913. From 1916 till her death in 1926, Bell worked for the British government, helping to set up the new country of Iraq.

Red Sea

N

W   E

S

The high Elburz Mountains in Iran, which Stark crossed to reach the Hashshashin castle at Alamut.

The travel writer

Freya Stark (1893–1993) developed a taste for traveling alone in the roughest, most remote areas. She learned Arabic and in 1927 set out for Arabia, traveling with the Bedouin. She wrote books about her many journeys, and said that "to awaken quite alone in a strange town is one of the most pleasant sensations in the world."

A lone traveler

Freya Stark was fascinated by the Hashshashin, a feared medieval Muslim sect. They carried out many daring missions to murder their enemies, and gave us our word *assassin,* meaning killer. Stark visited their castle at Alamut in northern Persia (now Iran) in 1930, and returned a year later to map the area. Stark traveled around the Arabian desert in the years that followed and continued to explore the Middle East until the 1950s.

Gertrude Bell

In 1892, Gertrude Bell (1868–1926) made her first visit to Persia (Iran), where her uncle served in the British embassy. She fell in love with the culture, and devoted most of her adult life to studying the Middle East.

Time Line

1899
Gertrude Bell tours Palestine and Syria

1909
Bell first visits Mesopotamia (now Iraq)

1913–14
Bell travels from Syria to Iraq and into Arabia

1916–26
Bell helps set up the new state of Iraq

1927–28
Freya Stark travels through Arabia

1928–32
Based in Baghdad, Stark travels extensively around the Middle East

1933–39
Stark travels alone in the Arabian desert

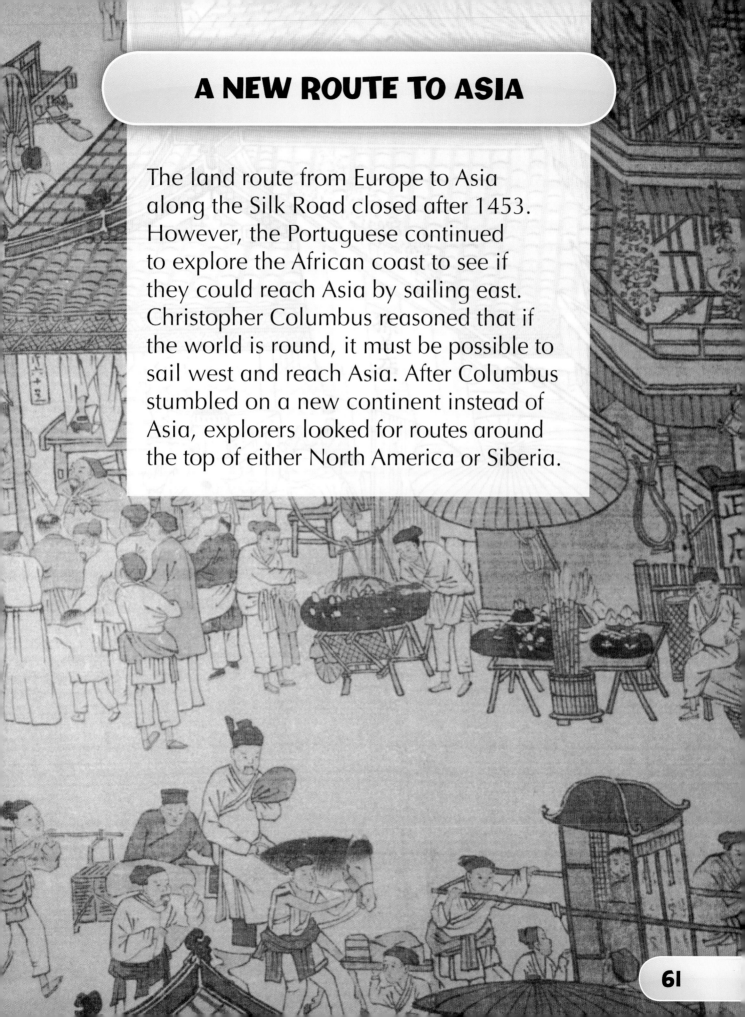

A NEW ROUTE TO ASIA

The land route from Europe to Asia along the Silk Road closed after 1453. However, the Portuguese continued to explore the African coast to see if they could reach Asia by sailing east. Christopher Columbus reasoned that if the world is round, it must be possible to sail west and reach Asia. After Columbus stumbled on a new continent instead of Asia, explorers looked for routes around the top of either North America or Siberia.

Columbus's first voyage

Italian Christopher Columbus dreamed of sailing west from Europe to reach Cipangu (Japan). In 1491, King Ferdinand and Queen Isabella of Spain agreed to fund his voyage.

The fleet

On August 3, 1492 Columbus set sail from the Spanish port of Palos with three ships: the three-masted cargo ship, *Santa Maria,* the three-masted caravel, the *Niña,* and the four-masted caravel, the *Pinta.* After a stop in the Canary Islands, the fleet set off again on September 6.

Columbus

Christopher Columbus (c.1451–1506) was born in the Italian port of Genoa. Remarkably little is know about his early life. In 1476, he moved to Lisbon and married a Portuguese noblewoman. He died in Spain in 1506.

It's a Mystery!

Columbus landed on an island he named San Salvador. Historians have suggested nine possible places in the Bahamas, but nobody really knows where Columbus landed.

Columbus's fleet, the *Niña,* the *Santa Maria* (center), and the *Pinta.*

The pineapple, one of many new foods eaten by Columbus.

New discoveries

Columbus did not find gold or rich trading cities in the lands he thought were Asia, but he and his crew did eat new foods, such as pineapples, potatoes, and corn. He also observed the Arawaks smoking tobacco leaves in a pipe.

A new world?

In the night of October 12, the lookout on the *Pinta* saw land. Columbus and crew landed on the island they named San Salvador and claimed it for Spain. Columbus was convinced he had landed off the west coast of India, so he named these islands the West Indies. He would never know he had discovered a continent that was previously unknown to Europeans.

Time Line

August 3, 1492
Columbus sets sail with three ships and a crew of 85 from Palos in Spain

October 12
Land is sighted two hours after midnight

October 28
Columbus reaches Cuba and sails along the coast before sailing to Hispaniola

December 25
While exploring the Hispaniola coastline, the *Santa Maria* runs aground and is abandoned

January 16, 1493
After establishing a colony in what is now Haiti, Columbus returns to Spain

The Arawaks

On San Salvador, Columbus traded glass beads with the native Arawaks in return for parrots and "a kind of dry leaf," tobacco. The Arawaks told him of a king to the south who had much gold, and Columbus set off to find him. The Arawaks soon died of diseases brought by Europeans, for which they had no immunity.

Arawak musicians danced as they played.

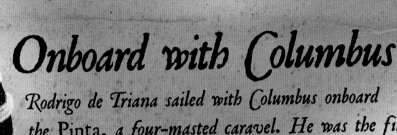

Onboard with Columbus

Rodrigo de Triana sailed with Columbus onboard the Pinta, a four-masted caravel. He was the first European since the Vikings to see the coast of the Americas, but his achievement went unrewarded. Columbus wrote his version of events in a diary. Here is the story from Rodrigo's point of view.

(Rodrigo de Triana is real. His diary is made up.)

Across the ocean

AUGUST 3, 1492 We left sight of Palos this day, and with it my beloved homeland of Spain. We are heading west. I trust my captain, Don Martin Alonso Pinzón, and the commander of our fleet, Don Christopher Columbus, but I fear what lies ahead, for it is unknown. Don Christopher hopes to sail to Asia, and we can only pray that we arrive there safely.

AUGUST 13 We sight the islands of the Canaries, and I am relieved to see land again. We will wait here while the rudder of our ship is repaired and the Niña is given a new rig to make her safe to cross this great ocean.

SEPTEMBER 16 The sea around is suddenly full with tufts of bright green grass. There is so much seaweed that the ocean looks like a vast meadow. I think we must be near land, but I see none ahead. The wind is very light and blows, when it does, from all directions.

A false alarm

SEPTEMBER 26 Yesterday was a day I wish to forget. Just after high noon, I thought I saw land out to the west, and shouted the good news to my captain. But I was wrong, and I have been punished for my mistake.

OCTOBER 7 Flocks of birds fly past us overhead in the direction of the southwest. Don Christopher has given orders that we change direction to follow them.

Land ahoy!

OCTOBER 12 Last night Don Christopher thought he saw a light to the west that he said was "like a little wax candle bobbing up and down." Then, at two hours past midnight this morning, I spied land. This morning, Don Christopher and some crew, including me, landed on this isle. We christened it San Salvador.

Gulf of Mexico

San Salvador

Juana

Atlantic Ocean

Santiago

Hispanola

N
W — E
S

Caribbean Sea

San Juan Bautista

Cabot (right) departs from Bristol.

John Cabot

John Cabot, or Giovanni Caboto, was born in Italy in about 1450 and died around 1498. He settled in Bristol, England, where he hoped to find sponsors for his voyage. His son, Sebastian (1476–1557), was also a noted explorer.

The newfound land

When Columbus returned to Europe in 1493 with news of his "discovery" of a new route to Asia, other navigators quickly followed him. Italian sailor John Cabot decided to sail a shorter route.

Sailing north

Spices arriving in England via the Middle East were very expensive, so merchants were interested in finding a shorter route to the east. Cabot knew that the shortest route to Asia would be to sail across the Atlantic Ocean at as northerly a latitude as possible. He presented his proposals to Henry VII of England.

The Newfoundland coast, where Cabot probably landed in 1497.

The Wye Valley, the source of the oak used to build Cabot's ship, the *Matthew*.

A wealthy sponsor

Richard Amerike was a wealthy Welsh merchant who became Sheriff of Bristol in 1503. Amerike sponsored Cabot's two voyages, and some historians believe that Cabot named the new lands he found after his generous sponsor.

Canadian landfall

Henry VII agreed to support the voyage, so in 1497 Cabot set off from Bristol onboard the *Matthew*. He landed in North America, probably on the island of Newfoundland, or possibly farther south at Nova Scotia, both in modern-day Canada. In 1498, Cabot set off again, this time with five ships, but was never heard of again.

The replica of the *Matthew*.

The *Matthew*

Cabot's boat, the *Matthew*, was a three-masted ship. It weighed about 55 tons (50 tonnes), making it a relatively small ship. Built of oak, it carried a crew of about 18 sailors and, although small, was very seaworthy. In 1997, a replica was built in Bristol to celebrate the 500th anniversary of the *Matthew*'s voyage.

Time Line

1494 or 1495
Cabot settles in Bristol

May 1497
Cabot sails west

June 24, 1497
Makes landfall in either Newfoundland or Nova Scotia

August 6 1497
Returns to Bristol

May 1498
Cabot sets out on his second voyage and is never heard of again

What Next?

Cabot thought he had landed on an island off the coast of Asia. By 1502, it was called "the newfound land." and the name is still used for the Canadian province of Newfoundland.

Naming the continent

Although Columbus was convinced he had sailed to the "Indies," or Asia, others were unsure because the land was too close to Europe to be Asia. It was, in fact, a new continent previously unknown to Europeans.

Who was first?

In 1499–1500, four Europeans sailed to South America. Who arrived first is unclear, although many historians credit Pedro Cabral, who sighted Brazil on April 22, 1500. Vicente Pinzón reached the northeast of Brazil, possibly in January 1500. On a third expedition, Alonso de Ojeda explored the Caribbean coast, and Amerigo Vespucci sailed along the coast farther east.

Amerigo Vespucci

Amerigo Vespucci (1451–1512) was born in Florence in northern Italy. In 1491, Vespucci left for Seville in Spain, and in 1499, he joined the expedition led by Alonso de Ojeda (c.1468–1515).

Time Line

1499–1500
Ojeda sails along the Caribbean coast; Vespucci explores eastern Brazil

1500
Vicente Pinzón and Pedro Cabral land in Brazil

1501–02
Vespucci makes second voyage possibly reaching as far south as Patagonia in modern-day Argentina

What Next?

Portugal's territory in the new continent was named "Brasil," after a term used by Irish monks and seafarers for a legendary unknown land.

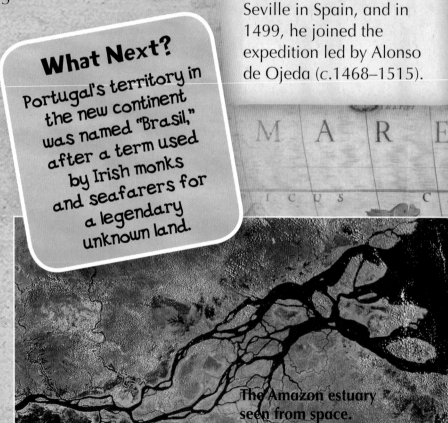

The Amazon estuary seen from space.

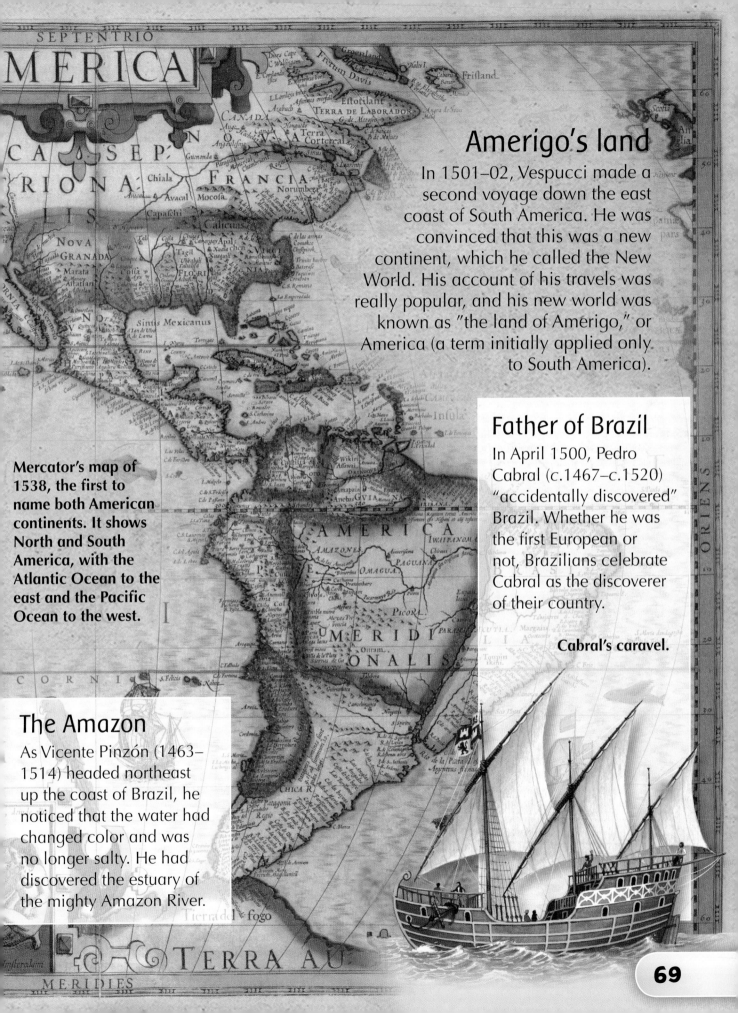

Amerigo's land

In 1501–02, Vespucci made a second voyage down the east coast of South America. He was convinced that this was a new continent, which he called the New World. His account of his travels was really popular, and his new world was known as "the land of Amerigo," or America (a term initially applied only to South America).

Mercator's map of 1538, the first to name both American continents. It shows North and South America, with the Atlantic Ocean to the east and the Pacific Ocean to the west.

Father of Brazil

In April 1500, Pedro Cabral (c.1467–c.1520) "accidentally discovered" Brazil. Whether he was the first European or not, Brazilians celebrate Cabral as the discoverer of their country.

Cabral's caravel.

The Amazon

As Vicente Pinzón (1463–1514) headed northeast up the coast of Brazil, he noticed that the water had changed color and was no longer salty. He had discovered the estuary of the mighty Amazon River.

East coasting

As Central America was explored, it soon became clear that there was no way through to Asia. But determined explorers continued to search for a passage to China and the east.

Under the French king

King Francis I of France asked Giovanni da Verrazano to explore the coastline of North America between Florida (claimed by Spain) and Newfoundland (claimed by England). Verrazano set out to find land to settle while still searching for a route to China.

Giovanni da Verrazano

Verrazano (c.1485–c.1528) was born in Italy but moved to Dieppe, France, to pursue a naval career. He made several voyages on behalf of the French king. He also became a successful corsair (pirate), raiding Spanish treasure ships returning from Central America.

It's Amazing!
Of Verrazano's four ships, only *La Dauphine* made the entire voyage. Two ships were wrecked. The third returned to France laden with captured Spanish treasure.

Verrazano traded with the Narragansett, whom he described as "the goodliest people."

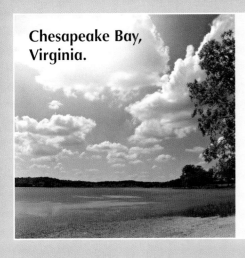
Chesapeake Bay, Virginia.

Chesapeake Bay

Verrazano mistook the vast inlet of Chesapeake Bay for "a strait through to the Eastern Ocean (Pacific)." He called it the Verrazano Sea. His mistake was only pointed out a century later.

Time Line

1524
Verrazano sets off for the New World with four ships; two are soon wrecked

March 1, 1524
Arrives off Cape Fear, North Carolina

April 1524
Enters Chesapeake Bay

April 17, 1524
Discovers New York Bay and then sails on to Narragansett Bay, where he spends two weeks exploring

May 5, 1524
Sails for Cape Cod and on to Newfoundland

July 8, 1524
Returns home to Dieppe

Mission accomplished?

Verrazano arrived off Cape Fear in North Carolina in March 1524. He sailed north to Chesapeake Bay, and then up the Delaware and New Jersey coasts to Rhode Island. Here, he spent two weeks in Narragansett Bay, trading with the local population. He continued up the coast to Newfoundland before sailing home across the North Atlantic. He believed he had found a sea route to Asia, and rich land on which to settle.

New York Harbor

As Verrazano sailed up the Atlantic coast, he discovered New York Bay. He anchored in the narrow entrance that today bears his name. He described the upper bay as a "pleasant lake" and named it Santa Margarita in honor of the king's sister.

The Verrazano-Narrows Bridge now stands at the mouth of New York Bay.

Martin Frobisher

The English adventurer Martin Frobisher (1539–94) first went to sea aged 13. His first voyage was a commercial expedition to Guinea in Africa. He soon became wealthy from piracy, seizing both Spanish and French ships.

The search for the northwest passage

By the middle of the 16th century, it was clear to European explorers that the American continent blocked the sea route west from Europe to Asia. The British attempted to sail through the northwest passage at the very top.

Ocean to ocean

The northwest passage starts in the North Atlantic Ocean and passes between Canada and Greenland into the Arctic Ocean. It then weaves its way between the various islands to the north of Canada before passing around Alaska into the Bering Sea and the northern Pacific Ocean. The main problem with this route is that it is ice-bound for much of the year.

An unfortunate hostage

Frobisher met some local Inuit in what is now Frobisher Bay. When five crew members disappeared, he accused the Inuit of kidnapping them and seized an Inuit to bargain with. When this got no response, he brought the Inuit and his canoe back to England. Sadly, the Inuit soon died of a cold.

An Inuit seal hunter in his canoe.

What Next?

In 1585, the English explorer John Davis made the first of three voyages to explore the northwest passage. He decided that there was no way through.

Fool's gold

The glittering rock that Frobisher discovered was brought back to England. He formed a company to exploit the mineral. However, the "gold" was, in fact, pyrite, a yellow, shiny mineral known as fool's gold. The company soon went bankrupt.

Fool's gold, made of sulfur, is used to make sulfuric acid.

A foolish mistake

In 1576, Martin Frobisher sailed from England past Iceland and Greenland across the Davis Strait to the south of Baffin Island. Here, he found an inlet—later named Frobisher Bay—around which lived Inuit, who he thought were Chinese. He then discovered glittering rocks he mistook for gold. Frobisher thought he had landed in Asia and found vast wealth, so he abandoned his quest, loaded up his ship with rocks, and returned home.

An Inuit igloo near Frobisher Bay.

Time Line

June 1576
Frobisher leaves the Shetland Isles

July 1576
Almost loses his ship, the *Gabriel*, in a storm off Greenland

August 11, 1576
Reaches Baffin Island; seizes an Inuit as a hostage

August 1576
Returns to England

1577
Sails to Frobisher Bay; returns with 220 tons (200 tonnes) of "gold"

1578
Leads a big fleet of 15 ships via Greenland and finds the strait that leads into Hudson Bay

Henry Hudson's tragic voyage

One man, Henry Hudson (1570–1611), was obsessed with finding a northern route from Europe to Asia. He made four voyages in total, exploring both the northwest passage and the Arctic Ocean. He did not succeed, but a river, bay, and strait are all named after him.

What Next?

In 1670, Prince Rupert, cousin of Charles II of England, set up the Hudson's Bay Company to administer lands around Hudson Bay and develop its fur trade. The company was very successful.

Greenland

Hudson Bay

Labrador Sea

North America

1607 journey
1608 journey
1609 journey
1610 journey

Atlantic Ocean

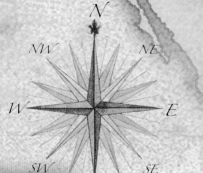

N
NW
NE
W
E
SW
SE
S

North and east

In 1607, the English Muscovy Company asked Henry Hudson to find a route across the North Pole to China. He sailed north up the coast of Greenland but polar ice stopped him. The following year, he headed along the north coast of Russia, again with no success.

East and west

In 1609, Hudson again searched for a northeast passage. He sailed around Scandinavia but then, with his crew close to mutiny, he turned around and sailed across the Atlantic, along the American coastline in search of a passage to Asia. The next year he set out to find the northwest passage.

The Hudson River in fall.

The Hudson River

On September 3, 1609 Henry Hudson sailed into New York Bay. He sailed up the river as far as Albany, only to discover that what he hoped might be a northwest passage was in fact merely a river.

Svalbard

Novaya Zemlya

Finland

Sweden

Norway

Europe

Amsterdam

London

eland

Time Line

1607
Hudson searches for a route across the North Pole to China, and is stopped by ice

1608
Hudson fails to find a northeast passage around Russia

1609
Hudson heads west after his crew mutinies on a voyage east

1610
Hudson searches for a northwest passage; he finds the bay that now bears his name, but is forced to winter in the bay when it freezes

1611
After a mutiny, Hudson is cast adrift and dies

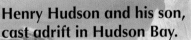

Henry Hudson and his son, cast adrift in Hudson Bay.

Cast adrift

On his final voyage, Hudson's ship became trapped in ice in what is now known as Hudson Bay. He was forced to spend the winter there. In spring, his crew mutinied and set Hudson, his son, and seven loyal sailors adrift in a small boat. Their fate is unknown.

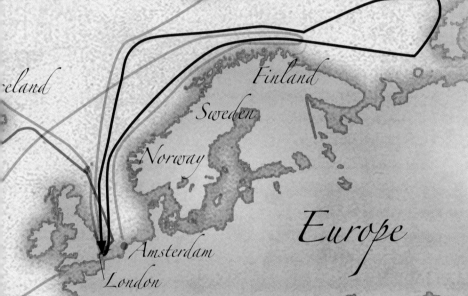

John Franklin

Sir John Franklin (1786–1847) was past retirement age when he led his polar expedition. He was, however, vastly experienced. A veteran of two previous Arctic voyages, he was well qualified to lead a major expedition.

The fatal expedition

The quest for a northwest passage from Europe to Asia continued during the 18th and 19th centuries, but ice around the Arctic islands remained solid almost year round. In 1845, the British Navy sent a major expedition to settle the matter.

Frozen ice

The expedition was led by Sir John Franklin, an experienced explorer. His fleet sailed up Baffin Bay between Greenland and Canada and then headed west through Lancaster Sound at the top of Baffin Island. Here he was iced in and forced to stay put for the winter.

Franklin's crews attempt to free their icebound ships.

King William Island

In 1857, Francis McClintock led a search for Franklin onboard the *Fox*. On King William Island, they found a tin cylinder buried in a mound of stones. Inside the tin was a document that explained what had happened to Franklin and his team.

Reindeer, a source of meat in summer on King William Island.

Time Line

May 1845
Franklin's expedition leaves England

1846–47
Expedition trapped in ice by King William Island and spends second Arctic winter there

1847
Franklin dies

1848
Remaining members of expedition walk south but die en route

Death on the ice

The next year, 1846, the expedition headed south to avoid the pack ice, finally reaching clear water near King William Island. Once again, however, the pack ice closed in, and Franklin and his team were forced to spend another winter in the Arctic. This time they did not survive, but died one by one from exposure.

What Next?

At least 40 expeditions searched for Franklin. Even more men and ships were lost looking for him than were lost in the expedition itself.

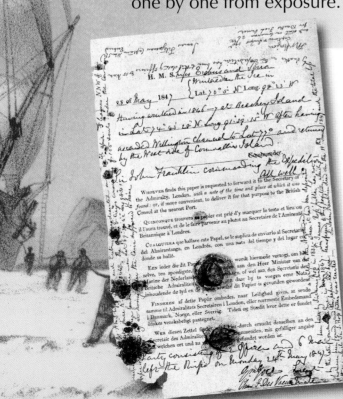

Franklin's last note

This note, found by the search mission of 1857, was signed by two of Franklin's officers. It records Franklin's death on June 11, 1847 and the fact that, after the expedition's two ships had been stuck in ice for over a year, the crews had abandoned ship and tried to reach safety by traveling south overland during 1848. None of them survived the journey.

77

Success at last

The numerous rescue missions that set out to find Franklin produced enough information to map the entire northwest passage. The Suez Canal opened in 1869, allowing ships to travel quickly between Europe and Asia. But one man still wanted to conquer the northwest passage.

Roald Amundsen

When he was just 15, Roald Amundsen (1872–1928) decided to become a polar explorer. He was the first person to sail through the northwest passage and the first to reach the South Pole.

Following Franklin

In 1903, Norwegian explorer Roald Amundsen decided to sail the passage, if only to prove it could be done. He sailed with a crew of only six but enough provisions to last for five years. He followed Sir John Franklin's route, even staying at one of his camps. The team then spent two winters on King William Island, before setting off again in August 1905.

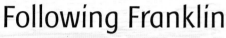

An Inuit sled pulled by huskies, a form of transport Amundsen learned to value.

Help from the locals

During their three winters in the Arctic, Amundsen and his team learned much from the local Inuit people. Lessons included how to handle dog sleds, how to catch fish and other food, and most importantly, how to survive the intense cold. During their third winter, the team received help from American whalers.

Time Line

June 1903
Amundsen sails from Oslo on the *Gjøa*

August 1903
Reaches Franklin's camp off Erebus Bay

September 1903
Makes camp on King William Island and spends two winters there

August 1905
Sets sail east toward the Beaufort Sea

September 1905
As the ice closes in, forced to spend another winter in the Arctic

October 1906
After breaking free of the ice, the *Gjøa* reaches San Francisco

What Next?

Global warming has caused the ice to recede dramatically. In 2007, this thaw fully opened up the northwest passage for the first time.

Patience is rewarded

As Amundsen sailed between King William Island and the mainland toward the Barents Sea, he met a ship from the Bering Strait sailing east, toward him. Success was almost on hand, but the ice soon closed in again and the team had to spend a third winter in the Arctic. The next year, Amundsen set off again, arriving to a hero's welcome in San Francisco. The northwest passage from the Atlantic to the Pacific Ocean had been conquered.

The *Gjøa*, a converted Norwegian fishing boat Amundsen used to sail the Arctic Ocean.

The Arctic Ocean

The ice cap that covers most of the Arctic Ocean grows bigger during the winter and recedes during the summer. However, the old theory that 24-hour summer sunshine might melt the ice was wrong. The sun's warming rays are reflected back by the white ice, keeping the Arctic Ocean permanently frozen around the North Pole.

The northeast passage

Like its northwest equivalent, no one was sure if the northeast passage around the top of Russia existed, and if it did, whether ice always blocked the route. During the 16th century, English and Dutch ships explored the north Russian coast.

Opening up Russia

The first people to explore this route were the English. In 1553, three ships sailed north to find a new route to China. Two became trapped in ice and the entire crew died. The other, commanded by Richard Chancellor (c.1520–56), failed to reach China but did sail into the White Sea to Archangel. From there he traveled overland to Moscow, capital of Ivan the Terrible's Russia.

Spitsbergen, discovered by Barents, became a lucrative source of whales, walruses, and seals.

What Next?

Chancellor's journey to Moscow opened up trade between England and Russia. In 1557, The Muscovy Company sent a mission to the Caspian Sea, establishing trade links between England and Persia.

Ivan the Terrible, seated center, welcomes an English trader to his court.

Ivan the Terrible

Ivan the Terrible (1530–84) was the first ruler to take the title Czar, or emperor, of Russia. His Russian nickname *grozny* better translates as "awe-inspiring" instead of "terrible," but he did have a violent, unpredictable nature. Ivan did much to expand Russian territory and introduced a number of reforms.

Time Line

1553
Three ships leave England to find a northeast passage to China; two ships are lost

1554
Richard Chancellor treks overland to Moscow

1594
Barents makes his first voyage to find the northeast passage and reaches Novaya Zemlya

1596
On his third expedition, Barents discovers Spitsbergen; he is iced in for the winter

June 1597
Barents dies just as the ice is beginning to melt; his crew is rescued

The hut Barents and his crew built from the wreck of their ship.

Barents' hut

In August 1596, Barents' ship was iced in and crushed. The crew used the wood to build a cabin in which to survive the winter, and as fuel for heating and cooking.

Willem Barents

The Dutch explorer Willem Barents (c.1550–97) made three attempts to find a sea route to China. Twice he reached Novaya Zemlya—a large island stretching from Siberia up into the Arctic Ocean—but was stopped by ice. On his third mission, Barents could see clear water beyond the island but was soon iced in. He died before he could be rescued.

Bear necessities

Barents and his crew saw many new things on their expeditions. On Bear Island to the south of Spitsbergen, they fought a polar bear, and named the island they had discovered after it. They felt ill after eating the bear, so chose not to hunt them. This was just as well because polar bear meat contains potentially deadly levels of vitamin A.

Polar bears were a constant danger to Arctic explorers.

Around Eurasia

Russian exploration of Siberia during the 18th century (see pages 48–51) meant that the Arctic northeast passage was relatively well known by the later 19th century. It just remained for someone to sail it.

(see pages 48–51)

What Next?

With the construction of powerful icebreakers during the 20th century, the northeast passage has become a major international waterway.

Planning success

Finnish explorer Adolf Nordenskiöld (1832–1901) worked out that the great rivers of Siberia must send enough warmish water north into the Arctic Ocean during the summer months to keep its coastal waters largely free of ice. He hoped to sail through the northeast passage by hugging the coastline.

Barents Sea

SWEDEN

FINLAND

NORWAY

RUSSIA

○ Karlskrona

UNITED KINGDOM

EUROPE

FRANCE

ITALY

SPAIN

Mediterranean Sea

ATLANTIC OCEAN

Suez Canal

AFRICA

SAUDI ARABIA

INDIAN OCEAN

The *Vega*, a powerful ice-resistant ship.

The *Vega*

Nordenskiöld's ship, the *Vega,* was a whaling ship. The hull was made of oak and had an outer layer of tougher wood to resist the ice. In addition to her sails, she also had a steam engine.

Success at last

ARCTIC OCEAN

Leaving from southern Sweden on the *Vega*, Nordenskiöld hugged the coast, and was less than 125 miles (200 km) from Cape Dezhnev at the eastern end of Siberia when he was iced in for the winter. When the ice cleared the following summer, he sailed around Asia to circumnavigate the entire Eurasian landmass.

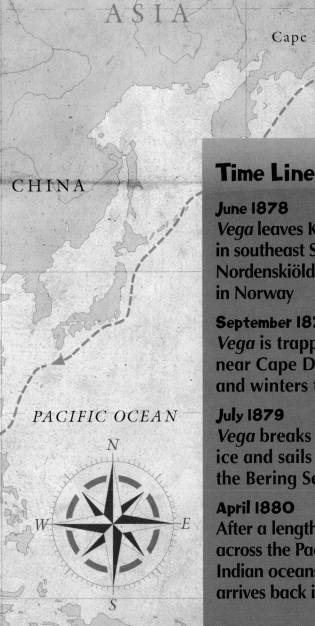

Bering Strait

ASIA

Cape Dezhnev

Bering Sea

Today, the Chukchi live in permanent settlements.

The Chukchi

The hardy Chukchi people of northeastern Siberia were traditionally divided into coastal hunters and inland reindeer herders who moved with their herds. The Chukchi helped Nordenskiöld and his men during their winter stay.

CHINA

INDIA

Bay of Bengal

South China Sea

PACIFIC OCEAN

N

W   E

S

INDONESIA

Time Line

June 1878
Vega leaves Karlskrona in southeast Sweden; Nordenskiöld boards in Norway

September 1878
Vega is trapped by ice near Cape Dezhnev and winters there

July 1879
Vega breaks free of the ice and sails south into the Bering Sea

April 1880
After a lengthy voyage across the Pacific and Indian oceans, the *Vega* arrives back in Sweden

Opening up Japan

One of the countries Columbus and other Europeans wanted to reach in Asia was the island empire of Japan. But European contact with the country was limited, and for a long time Japan shut its doors to all foreign visitors.

Religion and trade

The Portuguese first visited Japan in 1542 and were soon followed by the Jesuits. In 1609, the Dutch East India Company established a trading base near Nagasaki. In 1638, following the Shimabara rebellion, a 37,000-strong Japanese Christian army was massacred at Hara castle. Soon after, Portuguese traders were expelled. Only the Dutch and Chinese were allowed to continue to trade with Japan while the country closed itself off from the rest of the world.

Time Line

1542
First Portuguese traders arrive on Tanegashima

1639
Traders expelled from Japan; isolation begins

1853
First visit by United States fleet led by Perry

1854
Perry forces Japan to sign treaty with U.S.A.

1867
Japan begins process of modernization

Himeji Castle, in Kansai, has survived Japan's many wars unharmed.

Tokugawa Ieyasu, shogun of Japan.

The English samurai

William Adams (1564–1620) was the first Englishman to visit Japan in 1600. Imprisoned at first, he was later employed by the local lord to help build a modern navy. Made a samurai, or knight, he became a trusted advisor to Tokugawa Ieyasu, the shogun, or leading military ruler of Japan.

Gunboat diplomacy

During the 19th century, the United States became a major Pacific power. In 1853, the U.S. government sent a naval expedition to force the Japanese to negotiate and trade. Led by Commodore Matthew Perry, the fleet entered the port of Uraga in 1853 and returned the following year to Edo Bay with a squadron of warships. Faced with such military might, the Japanese caved in.

A samurai warrior in full armor.

It's Amazing!

Within 50 years, Japan used western technology to build a navy capable of beating the Russian imperial fleet.

The shogunate

Although Japan was supposedly ruled by its divine emperor, real power lay in the hands of the shogun. These military leaders continued to rule Japan until they were overthrown in 1867–68 and power was given back to the emperor.

The samurai rebels

Restored to power in 1867, the emperor embarked on a process of modernization. Not everybody was happy about this and the samurai warriors of the Satsuma clan were massacred in a battle with the new Japanese army in 1877.

Satsuma rebels surrender to government forces.

SAILING AROUND THE WORLD

The first explorers set off around the world in search of trade and plunder. Later, explorers increasingly sailed for scientific knowledge. In more recent years, people have sailed around the world for pleasure and adventure. Today, it is thought of as a sport. The ultimate test for any sailor is a solo voyage against the clock and against the worst the elements can throw at them.

The impossible voyage

Ferdinand Magellan didn't mean to sail around the world and, in fact, he didn't, because he died half way around. But his voyage is forever associated with the first circumnavigation of the world and was a remarkable feat of exploration.

Ferdinand Magellan

Magellan (c.1480–1521) was born in Portugal. He moved to Spain in 1517 to work for the Spanish king. Magellan was a skilled navigator and leader, demanding much of his men and even more of himself.

A new route to Asia

Magellan set out to do what Columbus had tried 27 years earlier—sailing west to find a sea route to Asia. With five Spanish ships, he set out in 1519 in search of the Spice Islands in Indonesia. He sailed south down the Atlantic, then wintered in Patagonia (southern Argentina).

An old map showing the Strait of Magellan, at the tip of South America, which connects the Atlantic and Pacific oceans.

Battle of Mactan

In the Philippines, Magellan tried to convert the local chiefs to Christianity. When the chief of Mactan refused, Magellan set out to punish him. Magellan was killed when the chief and his army attacked him and his men.

Magellan was killed by blows to the arm and the right leg.

Guam

The island of Guam is one of the Mariana Islands. The Spanish called the islands the Ladrones, the Spanish word for "thieves," because the islanders stole everything they could. But they gave Magellan fresh water, coconuts, and rice to feed his crew.

Guam is dotted with these "latte" stones—the remains of ancient houses.

Across the Pacific

Magellan sailed through the strait that now bears his name into the Pacific Ocean. As he crossed the ocean, his fleet ran out of food, but they reached Guam in March 1521. Here they took on provisions and set off for the Philippines, where Magellan hoped to convert the people to Christianity. He was killed the following month.

What Next?

Magellan claimed the Philippines as Spanish territory and they remained so until 1898. The Philippines became the only Christian nation in Asia.

Time Line

September 10, 1519
Magellan sets sail from Spain with five ships

March/April 1520
Winters in Patagonia and puts down a revolt by one his captains

November 1520
Sails through the Strait of Magellan into the Pacific Ocean

March 6, 1521
Reaches Guam

March 16, 1521
Arrives in the Philippines

March 28, 1521
Magellan's servant talks to the locals in his own language, proving to Magellan that he had reached Asia

April 27, 1521
Magellan killed on Mactan Island

The voyage home

Soon after Magellan's death, the remaining voyagers elected João Lopes Carvalho as their leader. Carvalho burned one of the three ships, destroyed Magellan's records, and for the next four months raided any passing ship for loot.

The *Victoria*, the only ship to make it home.

The new leader

Juan Sebastián Delcano (*c*.1492–1526) was the Basque seaman who completed Magellan's voyage. He showed that travelers who sailed west around the world lost a day by the time they came home, due to the rotation of the Earth.

Homeward bound

When Carvalho failed to find the Spice Islands, command was given to Juan Delcano. He discovered the spice-rich islands and then sailed home west to Spain. On board the *Victoria*, Delcano reached Spain in September 1522. With him were only 17 out of the original 250 European men, plus four East Indians.

Atlantic Ocean

EUROPE

Spain

AFRICA

It's a Mystery!

When Magellan came out of the Strait of Magellan into the new ocean, he found it to be "calm and benevolent," so he named it the Pacific Ocean.

Pacific Ocean

SOUTH AMERICA

Strait of Magellan

The great voyage

Although he did not live to enjoy it, Magellan's voyage was a huge achievement. He had discovered a westerly route to Asia and sailed across the Pacific Ocean, showing Europeans just how big the world was. He had also opened up new trade possibilities in the Philippines and Spice Islands, as well as discovering a whole new world of Pacific islands to be explored—and exploited—by Europeans.

Spices such as these were widely available in Asia.

Spice trade

Spices were highly valued in Europe for flavoring meat, after it had been salted, to preserve it. They were also used to flavor drinks. Among those found in the Spice Islands were pepper, cloves, and nutmeg.

Time Line

May 1521
Carvalho is elected leader a few days after Magellan is killed in battle

October 1521
After failing to find the Spice Islands, the remaining crew get rid of Carvalho and give command to Delcano

November 1521
Delcano finds the Spice Islands and sails for home in the *Victoria*, leaving the *Trinidad* behind for repairs

April 1522
The *Trinidad* returns to the Spice Islands and is held captive by the Portuguese

September 6, 1522
Delcano reaches Spain

Magellan killed

Philippines

Pacific Ocean

Indian Ocean

Spice Islands

Southern Ocean

The pirate adventurer

After the successful voyage of Magellan and Delcano, ships sailed to the Philippines and Spice Islands, but none circumnavigated the world. Francis Drake, an English adventurer and pirate, was the next to attempt such a voyage in 1577, sponsored by Queen Elizabeth I.

Raiding the Spanish

As relations between England and Spain grew hostile in the 1570s, Francis Drake planned to attack the Spanish in the Pacific Ocean. In 1577, he set sail with five ships. He raided Spanish treasure ships in the Pacific, capturing 80 pounds (36 kg) of gold.

A replica of the *Golden Hind* built in 1977 to mark the 400th anniversary of Drake's voyage.

Francis Drake

Drake (*c*.1540–96) was born in Tavistock, Devon. He was a skilled navigator and seaman and England's most famous pirate. He played a key role in defeating the Spanish Armada in 1588.

The Atlantic slave trade

Francis Drake's relative John Hawkins took slaves from West Africa to the West Indies. He sold them for goods, which he then sold in England. In 1566, Drake took part in one such voyage, narrowly escaping when the Spanish attacked.

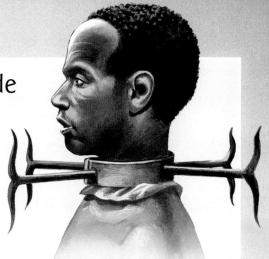

Slaves were transported in neck irons. Many died on the way.

A wealthy return

By now reduced to just his flagship, the *Golden Hind*, Drake stopped for repairs just north of modern-day San Francisco. He claimed the area for England. He then crossed the Pacific Ocean to the Spice Islands, where he loaded up with spices. He sailed for home with a huge treasure.

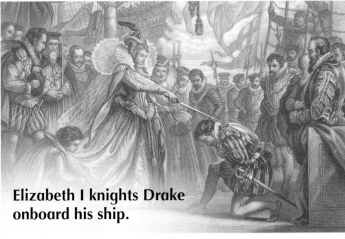

Elizabeth I knights Drake onboard his ship.

Arise, Sir Francis

When Drake returned home in 1580, Queen Elizabeth I did not at first acknowledge his achievement, because she did not want to upset the Spanish. However, she soon changed her mind, threw a banquet onboard the *Golden Hind,* and knighted Francis Drake.

Time Line

December 13, 1577
Drake leaves Plymouth with five ships

April 1578
Sails past eastern Brazil

August 24, 1578
Reaches Strait of Magellan

September 7, 1578
Reaches the Pacific, but is forced to sail 100 miles (160 km) south of Cape Horn

June 1579
Sails as far north as Vancouver Island

July 25, 1579
Starts voyage across the Pacific

September 26, 1580
Arrives home in Plymouth

Sailing with Drake

John Herbert sailed with Drake around the world.
Here is a fictional account of his voyage.

The voyage south

MAY 23, 1578 I sail onboard the Pelican with Master
Drake, a skilled seaman from my county of Devon. He has
been commanded by our majesty, Queen Elizabeth,
to attack the Spanish, but he did not tell us we
were bound for the Pacific Ocean until we
were well at sea. Our fleet has lost two
ships already in the South Atlantic,
and the Mary was abandoned
because it was found to be full of rot.

AUGUST 21, 1578 Our three ships passed
through the Strait of Magellan and into the
Pacific. A mighty gale blew us far south and east, so
that we sailed back into the Atlantic. And so we proved
that these two oceans meet at the far south.
Our master has renamed the Pelican the
Golden Hind, in honour of his patron,
Sir Christopher Hatton. There is a hind
(female deer) on Sir Christopher's coat of arms.

Raiding the seas

NOVEMBER 1578 We are now on our own in the Golden Hind, because we have lost a ship to the storm and the Elizabeth has returned home. But we are rich, for twice we have seized ships of Spain, and have raided their towns on the shore. We gave chase to the Cacafuego bound for Panama, and took 80 pounds of gold, including a crucifix of solid gold, as well as 13 chests full of gold bullion and much silver and jewels.

JUNE 17, 1579 We landed today in a place we do not know, but there are no Spanish here to detain us. Master Drake has claimed the land for the crown of England, and has named it Nova Albion for New Britain. The native people are friendly, and we plan to stay here to repair our ships. From here we will head north again to search for a passage around this land to the Atlantic Ocean. Then, I hope, we will return home at last.

Arctic Ocean

NORTH AMERICA

Atlantic Ocean

ASIA

Pacific Ocean

AFRICA

SOUTH AMERICA

Indian Ocean

AUSTRALIA

ANTARCTICA

Around and around and around

After Drake, the number of people circumnavigating the globe remained very small. The Englishman Thomas Cavendish completed the voyage in 1586–88, as did a few unknown traders and pirates. However, William Dampier sailed around the world not once, but three times.

Raiding and exploring

William Dampier was an adventurer. In the 1670s, he joined a pirate ship. He worked in a logging camp on the Gulf of Mexico, but lost his fortune when a hurricane destroyed the lumber. He sailed up and down the Pacific coast raiding Spanish ships, and in 1686 guided a ship across the Pacific. Dampier then sailed south to the northwest coast of New Holland (as Australia was then called), before returning to England in 1691.

Time Line

1676
Dampier joins a logging camp in Gulf of Mexico

1677–78
Starts raiding Spanish shipping and settlements

1686
Crosses the Pacific

1688
Lands in Australia

1691
Returns to England

1699–1701
Commands HMS *Roebuck* and is shipwrecked

1703–7
Sails around the world as a pirate

1708–10
Completes third circumnavigation

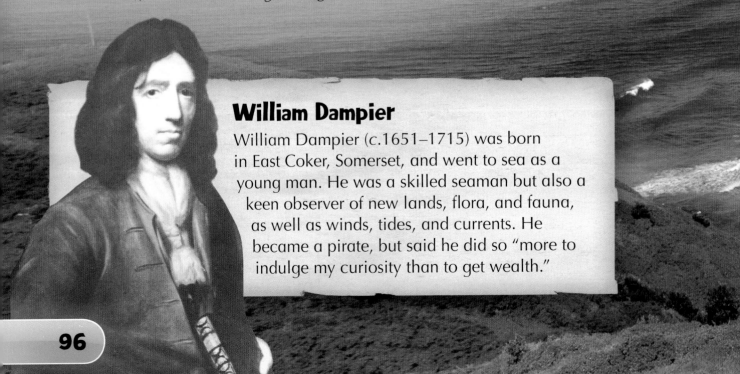

William Dampier

William Dampier (c.1651–1715) was born in East Coker, Somerset, and went to sea as a young man. He was a skilled seaman but also a keen observer of new lands, flora, and fauna, as well as winds, tides, and currents. He became a pirate, but said he did so "more to indulge my curiosity than to get wealth."

Around twice more

In 1703, Dampier set out again, this time as a licensed pirate. He was less successful than before, letting a Spanish treasure galleon slip away. He was jailed in the Dutch East Indies for piracy, and returned home only in 1707. A year later he set out again, this time as a pilot on two pirate ships. They roamed the Pacific Ocean with great success, although Dampier received little reward for his efforts.

The northwest coast of Australia, twice visited by William Dampier.

Some of the many drawings of animals and plants in Dampier's books.

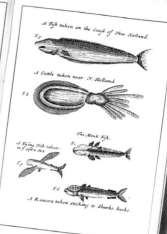

Dampier's account

Dampier wrote a book about his adventures. *A New Voyage Round the World* was published in 1697 and became a bestseller. Other books followed, with many valuable charts and surveys about the Pacific Ocean.

There is very little life on the rocky Ascension Island, but green turtles like this one lay their eggs there.

Ascension Island

In 1698, Dampier commanded HMS *Roebuck* on an expedition to find the supposed southern continent. On his way home, he was shipwrecked on Ascension Island in the Atlantic and was stuck there for five weeks before he and his crew were rescued.

It's Amazing!

In 1704, Dampier argued with one of his crew, Alexander Selkirk, and left him on an uninhabited island near Chile. Dampier's ship rescued him in 1709. Selkirk's adventures were the inspiration for Daniel Defoe's *Robinson Crusoe*.

Press gangs

In the 18th century, about one third of all men in the British Royal Navy had been forced into service by naval press gangs, which were authorized to force men into going to sea. Among Anson's crew were retired men drafted into naval service.

A man is dragged off by a press gang.

George Anson

Many of those who had circumnavigated the world in the 16th and 17th centuries were adventurers or pirates. George Anson was a naval commander acting on British government orders.

Attacking the Spanish

In 1740, Britain and Spain were at war. The British government ordered Anson to sail with seven ships to raid Spanish settlements on the Pacific coast of South America. Three of his ships were lost or turned back before he reached Cape Horn but Anson continued into the Pacific Ocean, inflicting great damage on Spanish shipping in the region.

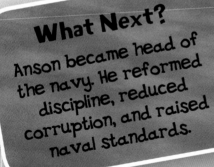

What Next?

Anson became head of the navy. He reformed discipline, reduced corruption, and raised naval standards.

The ruins of St. Paul's Cathedral in Macao, a Portuguese colony from 1557 to 1999.

Sealing his fortune

After Anson captured 32 wagonloads of treasure from *Nuestra Señora de Covadonga* in 1743, he needed somewhere to sell it. He chose the Portuguese colony of Macao, where he sold the loot to Chinese traders. Anson returned home a very rich man.

Anson's flagship the *Centurion* (left) attacks a Spanish treasure ship.

Golden success

With his own ships damaged, Anson consolidated all his crew onto one ship—his flagship *Centurion*—and crossed the Pacific to Macao on the Chinese coast. From here, he sailed out to capture a Spanish treasure galleon, *Nuestra Señora de Covadonga,* as it sailed from the Philippines to Mexico, seizing its loot.

Drawing the journey

Brett made drawings of sea lions such as these.

Piercy Brett, a lieutenant with Anson, kept a record of their journey by making drawings of what they saw. He drew many of the animals that they encountered along the way.

Time Line

September 18, 1740
Anson leaves England with seven ships

June 1741
Reaches Juan Fernández Islands off Chile with just four ships

1742
Reaches Macao with only one ship

June 20th, 1743
Captures *Nuestra Señora de Covadonga* off the Philippines

1744
Returns to England

John Byron, the record breaker

John Byron entered the record books when he completed the fastest circumnavigation yet recorded, sailing around the world in less than two years. This was not what he set out to do, however, so his voyage was considered a failure at the time.

Disobeying orders

Byron was put in command of a naval voyage to find and claim new lands in the South Atlantic. He set sail in 1764 onboard the *Dolphin* and reached the Falkland Islands. He then entered the Pacific but, instead of obeying orders to sail north, he sailed west.

Northern Mariana Islands

Gilbert Islands (Kiribati)

Batavia (Jakarta)

Tokelau

Indian Ocean

Australia

N
NW   NE
W   E
SW   SE
S

John Byron

British-born Byron (1723–86) joined the navy in his teens. He served under George Anson and fought the French in 1758. After his circumnavigation, he became governor of Newfoundland.

King penguins, one of five species of penguin on the Falkland Islands.

New claims

Byron claimed the Falkland Islands in the South Atlantic for Britain. He also claimed islands he found in the Pacific. He failed to anchor in one group of Tuamotu islands, which he named the Disappointment Islands. He named an island in the Gilbert Islands after himself!

Fast passage home

When he reached Batavia (now Jakarta) in Indonesia, Byron decided to head straight for home. He made a quick passage to Cape Town and sped up the Atlantic for Britain, which he reached in May 1766. He had set a world record and found islands in the Pacific, but had found no new Atlantic lands or any sea passages.

Time Line

June 21, 1764
Byron leaves Plymouth

1765
Reaches the Falkland Islands and claims them for Britain just as a French fleet claims them for France

April 1765
Enters the Pacific and discovers the Tuamotu, Tokelau, and Gilbert (now Kiribati) islands

November 1765
Reaches Batavia, now called Jakarta

May 9, 1766
Returns to Plymouth after a voyage lasting 22 months, 18 days

South America

South Atlantic Ocean

Tuamotu Islands

Pacific Ocean

Falkland Islands

New colonies

In 1763, France lost its American and Indian empires to Britain. The French government decided to send a naval expedition to the South Seas to find new lands to colonize.

The South Seas

The expedition, led by Louis-Antoine de Bougainville, arrived in the South Pacific in 1768. Bougainville claimed the Tuamotu Islands for France and then sailed on to Tahiti, which he also claimed. Here, he took onboard Ahu-toru, a chieftain's son who wanted to visit France. Laden with new supplies, Bougainville sailed west through the Society Islands, Samoa, and the New Hebrides (now Vanuatu).

It's Amazing!

During the voyage, it was discovered that one of the crew, the servant Jeanne Baré, was in fact a woman disguised as a man.

Louis-Antoine de Bougainville

Bougainville (1729–1811) studied law and mathematics before going to sea. He served in Canada as aide-de-camp to General Montcalm, who lost Quebec to the British in 1759, when he organized the evacuation of French troops. After his circumnavigation, he served as secretary to King Louis XV.

Time Line

January 1768
Bougainville's two ships pass through the Strait of Magellan into the Pacific Ocean

March 1768
Claims the Tuamotu islands for France

April 1768
Sails into Tahiti

June 4, 1768
Avoids shipwreck on the Great Barrier Reef

September 1768
Sails to Batavia

March 16, 1769
Arrives home in St. Malo

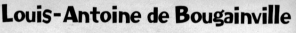

102

Missed opportunity

Bougainville rounded the Great Barrier Reef off Australia—missing the chance to claim the continent for France—and headed to the Dutch East Indies. He replenished his supplies and sailed across the Indian Ocean and back home to France. He had lost only seven out of more than 200 men (and one woman) while at sea.

A boat race in Tahiti, which Bougainville considered paradise.

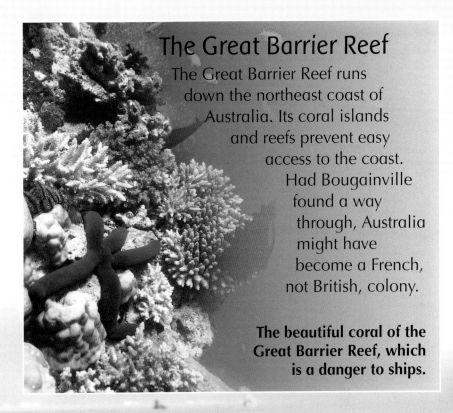

The Great Barrier Reef

The Great Barrier Reef runs down the northeast coast of Australia. Its coral islands and reefs prevent easy access to the coast. Had Bougainville found a way through, Australia might have become a French, not British, colony.

The beautiful coral of the Great Barrier Reef, which is a danger to ships.

Bougainvillea

Among the crew was botanist Philibert Commerçon, who recorded many new species. Among them was Bougainvillea, a brightly flowered tropical vine introduced to Europe by Bougainville and named after him.

Bougainvillea, a pretty vine from South America.

An American does it

Charles Wilkes was the first American to circumnavigate the globe. Along the way, he contributed to a vast increase in understanding of the world's oceans.

Sailing the oceans

In 1838, Wilkes was put in charge of the U.S. South Seas Exploring Expedition, designed to increase scientific and maritime knowledge. The fleet of six ships sailed south to Tierra del Fuego and on to the Antarctic. From there it sailed across the Pacific to Australia, back to the Antarctic, and then north via Hawaii to Oregon. It crossed the Pacific again to the East Indies, sailed across the Indian Ocean, and around the Cape of Good Hope, arriving in New York in 1842.

Time Line

August 18, 1838
Expedition departs and crosses the Atlantic

February 1839
Establishes a base on Tierra del Fuego

November 1839
Crosses the Pacific to Australia

January 19, 1840
First sights Antarctica

September 1840
Studies volcanoes in Hawaii

April 1841
Sails to Oregon coast

November 1841
Sails for home

August 9, 1842
Three remaining ships arrive in New York

Wilkes braved icebergs, such as this one, to land on Antarctica and take rock samples.

Charles Wilkes

Charles Wilkes (1798–1877), from New York City, joined the U.S. navy at the age of 18. He became interested in astronomy and surveying and an authority in hydrography—the science of the oceans, seas, lakes, and rivers. After the expedition ended, he prepared its many papers for publication.

The achievement

Wilkes's fleet crossed the Pacific Ocean three times and sailed more than 79,500 miles (128,000 km). It mapped the Oregon coast and 1,590 miles (2,560 km) of the Antarctic coastline, surveyed about 300 islands, and produced 180 navigational charts. Wilkes's achievements proved that the United States could mount an expedition comparable in size and ambition to those of Britain and France.

The guanaco, one of the animals on Tierra del Fuego.

What Next?

Wilkes's charting of the Oregon coastline and the Columbia River increased American interest in Oregon, at the time jointly run with Britain. In 1846, the territory joined the United States.

Tierra del Fuego

Wilkes's naturalists observed many animals on Tierra del Fuego, the island at the southern tip of South America. These included Magellan penguins and plovers, seals, wolves, guanacos, and foxes.

The three-masted *Vincennes*.

The *Vincennes*

The *Vincennes* was a 860-ton (780-tonne) sloop on which Wilkes spent most of the expedition. He started off with six ships, but most were too old for the expedition. Two were lost near Cape Horn and only half the fleet made it home.

Slocum preferred to sail by himself and wrote a bestseller called *Sailing Alone Around the World*.

Going solo

By the late 19th century, circumnavigations took place all the time, as steamships sailed the world carrying tea, coal, wheat, and other products. However, no one had ever sailed a yacht single-handed around the world. That prize went to a 54-year-old American sea captain.

Setting sail

After three years restoring his small yacht, the *Spray*, Joshua Slocum set sail from Boston, Massachusetts, in April 1895 and crossed the Atlantic to Gibraltar. He then sailed south via the Cape Verde Islands to Brazil, spending Christmas in Montevideo. He entered the Pacific Ocean through the Strait of Magellan.

The *Spray*

Slocum's boat, the *Spray,* was an ancient oysterman he first saw propped up in a field and covered with canvas. During 1893, he completely rebuilt her hull using white pasture oak. She was only 36¾ feet (11.2 m) long and 14 feet (4.3 m) wide, but she was very seaworthy and easy to sail single-handed.

A short cut

The opening of the Suez Canal in 1869 meant there was no need for yachts to sail around the Cape of Good Hope. Joshua Slocum did not take this route, however, choosing instead to spend the Christmas of 1897 in South Africa.

A steamship passes through the Suez Canal.

Alone around the world

Slocum crossed the Pacific to Australia, where he spent months sailing slowly down the east coast. He then headed north around the top of Australia and crossed the Indian Ocean to Cape Town, where he spent another Christmas. Next, he sailed via St. Helena and Ascension to northern Brazil and up to Rhode Island, arriving in June 1898. He had sailed a total distance of 46,000 miles (74,000 km) on his own. He wrote a best-selling book about his adventure.

Time Line

April 24, 1895
Slocum sets sail from Boston, Massachusetts

July 1895
Crosses the Atlantic to Gibraltar

December 1895
After sailing south, spends Christmas in Uruguay

1896
Cruises through the Pacific to Australia

1897
Cruises from Australia across the Indian Ocean

December 1897
Docks in Cape Town, South Africa

June 27, 1898
Arrives in Rhode Island

It's a Mystery!

In 1909, Joshua Slocum set out from Bristol, Rhode Island, bound for Grand Cayman in the Caribbean Sea and was never seen again. It is probable that a steamer ran him down when he was asleep belowdecks.

Lady Brassey wrote an account of her voyage.

Sailing in style

The first private yacht to circumnavigate the world was the *Sunbeam*, owned and skippered by Thomas Brassey, a British MP and later lord. The voyage lasted from July 1876 to May 1877. Brassey was accompanied by his wife and a crew of 32, which included a maid.

One-stop voyage

Gipsy Moth IV on a calm day.

Before the 1960s, all mariners wanting to sail single-handed around the world had to stop at numerous ports, because sailboats were slow and had to stop for supplies. New technology lets yachts sail faster and farther than ever.

Chichester leaves Plymouth to a relatively quiet send-off.

Leaving home

Francis Chichester left Plymouth's harbor in his boat, the *Gipsy Moth IV*, a two-masted ketch. He aimed to better the times achieved by the fastest clipper ships of the 19th century.

The record breaker

Englishman Francis Chichester (1901–72) was both a sailor and an aviator—he was the first man to fly solo eastwest across the Tasman Sea in 1931. In 1960, he became the first person to sail solo from east to west across the North Atlantic against the prevailing winds, setting a time of 40 days. In 1966, he set out to sail around the world, making only one stop.

Alone onboard

It takes huge stamina to sail a boat single-handed, because you must always keep a lookout for other boats. Hauling heavy sails or climbing the mast to make repairs requires strength. Loneliness, too, is a great problem.

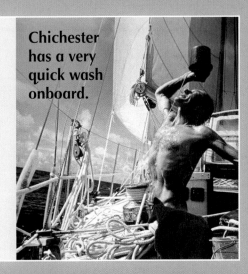

Chichester has a very quick wash onboard.

Via Sydney to home

The first leg of Chichester's voyage, from Plymouth, England, via the Cape of Good Hope to Sydney, Australia, took 107 days. After a six-week stop in Sydney, Chichester set off across the Pacific Ocean and around Cape Horn into the Atlantic and home to Plymouth. The return leg took 119 days. Chichester had sailed alone around the world in just 226 days at an average speed of 6 knots.

A hero's welcome

Thousands of small boats accompanied Gipsy Moth IV into Plymouth Sound on Chichester's return, letting off horns and sirens while fireboats sprayed red, white, and blue water. The Royal Artillery sounded a 10-gun salute. Soon afterward, Chichester received a knighthood from the Queen.

Sir Francis Chichester on the day he was knighted.

Time Line

August 27, 1966
Chichester leaves Plymouth onboard Gipsy Moth IV

December 12, 1966
After 107 days at sea, he arrives in Sydney, where he repairs the yacht and takes on new supplies

January 29, 1967
Leaves Sydney

May 28, 1967
Returns home to a hero's welcome in Plymouth

July 7, 1967
Receives a knighthood from the Queen in Greenwich

Racing around the world

After Francis Chichester's voyage, there was only one yachting record left—sailing single-handed around the world without stopping.

Alone, nonstop

In early 1968, five sailors prepared to face this challenge. The British *Sunday Times* newspaper sponsored the race. Each entrant had to start and finish at the same British port of their choosing and sail around the Cape of Good Hope and then Cape Horn. Only one entrant finished. Robin Knox-Johnston became the first person ever to circumnavigate the globe nonstop by himself.

Time Line

June 14, 1968
Robin Knox-Johnston leaves Falmouth, England, on board the ketch *Suhaili*

April 22, 1969
Knox-Johnston arrives back in Falmouth

2005
Ellen MacArthur sails round the world in *B&Q/Castorama* in a record 71 days

2005
Bruno Peyron and crew in *Orange II* sail round the world in under 51 days

2008
Francis Joyon sets new solo record of 57 days

It's Amazing!

The Jules Verne Trophy is awarded for the fastest circumnavigation of the world. The current record, set by Frenchman Bruno Peyron in 2005, is 50 days, 9 hours, 32 minutes, and 45 seconds!

Robin Knox Johnston

Knox-Johnston (born 1939) was the first person to sail single-handed around the world without stopping. He went around the world again in a crewed yacht in 1977 and won the Jules Verne Trophy for the fastest circumnavigation in 1994.

The fastest sailor alive

Solo circumnavigations have always been rare, but for a woman to attempt it is even rarer. British sailor Ellen MacArthur (born in 1976) came second in the Vendée Globe solo around-the-world race in 2001. In 2005, she sailed the trimaran *B&Q/Castorama* solo around the world in 71 days, breaking the record of Frenchman Francis Joyon by one day. Joyon took the record back in 2008, when he completed the voyage in just 57 days.

MacArthur's yacht, a crucial factor in her record-breaking voyage.

Ellen MacArthur in training for the 2001 Vendeé Globe race.

Record-breaking boat

The *B&Q/Castorama*, the boat on which Ellen MacArthur set her record, was a high-tech trimaran that was custom-built for her in Australia. Many of its components were designed to be ideally placed for a person of her height.

Natural hazards

Modern yachts use the Global Positioning System, a satellite-based system that tells you where you are. But you still need to keep a look out—it does not tell you when a whale is in your way!

A humpback whale surfaces. Underwater, it is a danger to sailors.

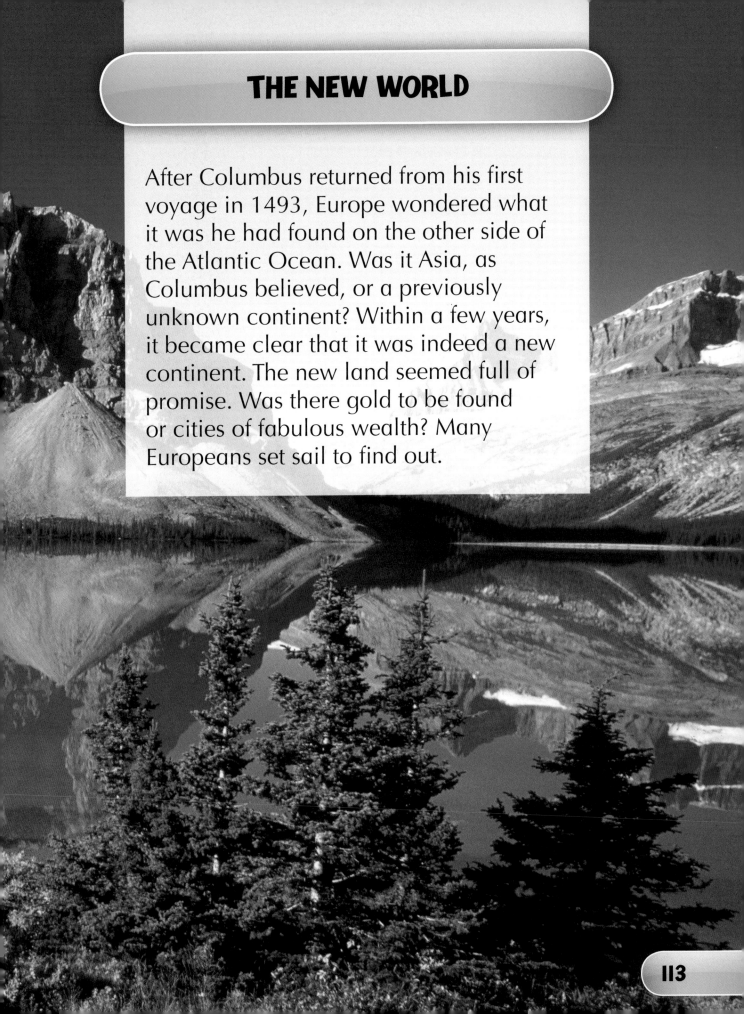

THE NEW WORLD

After Columbus returned from his first voyage in 1493, Europe wondered what it was he had found on the other side of the Atlantic Ocean. Was it Asia, as Columbus believed, or a previously unknown continent? Within a few years, it became clear that it was indeed a new continent. The new land seemed full of promise. Was there gold to be found or cities of fabulous wealth? Many Europeans set sail to find out.

The return of Columbus

After his first voyage in 1492–93, Columbus crossed the Atlantic Ocean three more times to explore the islands he had first visited. These voyages opened up the new continent to European explorers and conquerors.

Time Line

1493–96
On his second voyage, Columbus explores and names the Leeward Islands, and establishes a colony on Hispaniola

July 31, 1498
On his third voyage, Columbus lands on Trinidad before exploring mainland South America nearby

August 19, 1498
Returns to Hispaniola, where he is placed under arrest and then sent home

1502–4
Explores east coast of Central America, searching for a passage to the Indian Ocean

1506
Columbus dies

It's Amazing!

In 1494, Pope Alexander VI signed the Treaty of Tordesillas. He drew a line down a map of the Atlantic Ocean and divided the new world between the Spanish and Portuguese.

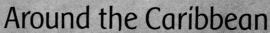
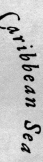

Caribbean Sea

Around the Caribbean

In 1493–96, Columbus made his second voyage, exploring the Caribbean and establishing a settlement on Hispaniola. On his third voyage in 1498, he became the first European to set foot on South America. He then returned to rule Santo Domingo. Following complaints, he was arrested by the new Spanish governor and sent to Spain for trial.

New settlers

The first Spanish settlements in the New World were established on the island of Hispaniola. The first colony, La Navidad, was destroyed by local Taíno people. Columbus set up a new colony at Santo Domingo, which is now the capital of the Dominican Republic.

A reconstructed Taíno village on Hispaniola.

Farther west

Columbus won his trial in Spain, and in 1502 he set out again. This time he headed west through the islands until he hit land. This was the Central American coastline, but Columbus thought he had found a route through to Asia.

CUBA

La Navidad

HISPANIOLA

Santo Domingo

JAMAICA

North Atlantic Ocean

LEEWARD ISLANDS

⟵ 2nd voyage (1493–96)

⟵ 3rd voyage (1498–1500)

⟵ 4th voyage (1502–4)

The Spanish Empire

The Spanish were very cruel to the native population, who rebeled against their rule. This, combined with new diseases, completely wiped out the native population of the Caribbean.

Hatuey, a Taíno leader, fought Spanish rule on Cuba and was burned alive after refusing to be baptized.

TRINIDAD

First steps on the mainland

From their settlements in the Caribbean, the Spanish set out to explore the North and Central American mainland that lay to their west. These explorations opened the way for Spanish colonization of the entire region.

The Pacific

In 1510, the Spanish explorer Vasco Núñez de Balboa (1475–1519) established the Spanish colony of Santa Maria La Antigua del Darien on the Panama isthmus in Central America. Here, he heard reports from the local people of a vast ocean to the west. In 1513, he crossed the isthmus and became the first European to see the Pacific Ocean.

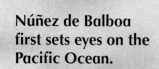

Núñez de Balboa first sets eyes on the Pacific Ocean.

Juan Ponce de León

The explorer Juan Ponce de León (c.1460–1521) colonized Puerto Rico and discovered Florida. Rare for his time, he believed in peaceful colonization. He showed kindness and friendship to the people he met.

It's a Mystery!

The Spanish were keen to explore the islands north of Cuba, which were rumored to contain a fountain that granted eternal youth if you washed in its waters.

Time Line

1510
Núñez de Balboa establishes first Spanish colony on mainland

March 1513
Ponce de León lands in a place he names Florida

September 27, 1513
Núñez de Balboa sights Pacific Ocean and claims it for Spain

1528
Cabeza de Vaca and three others are shipwrecked on the Texas coast, from where they embark on a long journey to safety

1542
Cabeza de Vaca's account of his adventures is published

The long trek

In 1513, Juan Ponce de León sailed north from Spanish Puerto Rico and landed in a place he called Tierra La Florida (Land of Flowers). Fifteen years later, a fleet set out to explore Florida, but it was shipwrecked in the Gulf of Mexico. Only a few men survived, among them Álvar Núñez Cabeza de Vaca (c.1490–1556), who wrote about his experiences. Aided by local Yaqui tribesmen, they walked 1,240 miles (2,000 km) to be rescued.

Yaqui territory

Cabeza de Vaca walked through the region that is now Texas. It was then inhabited by Yaqui and other native people. The Spanish conquered the area in the 1600s, and in 1821 it became Mexican territory. Texas declared its independence from Mexico in 1836 and became part of the United States nine years later.

A Yaqui dancer invoking the power of the spirit world.

Bison

While trekking through what is now Texas, Cabeza de Vaca met a group of local people who had gathered to harvest the prickly pear cactus. They also encountered a herd of hairy, hunch-backed cows grazing on the plains—the first bison ever seen by Europeans.

Cortés in Mexico

The people that explorers first encountered in the Americas were self-sufficient farmers and hunters. In European eyes, they were very primitive, but this view of the continent changed when the Aztec Empire of Mexico was discovered.

Into the interior

In 1518, the Spanish governor of Cuba sent 11 ships under the command of Hernán Cortés (1485–1547) to explore the coast of the Yucatán peninsula of Mexico. Once there, Cortés learned of a great inland empire and set out to find it. He marched inland with only a handful of men and horses, but soon found local allies willing to fight against their rulers, the Aztecs.

An Aztec map of Tenochtitlán.

Tenochtitlán

The Aztec capital housed perhaps 250,000 people—far more than any European city of the time. It ruled an empire of 10 million people from the Pacific to the Caribbean.

An Aztec calendar, based on a complex cycle of 20-day periods.

The Aztecs

The Aztecs settled in central Mexico in the 13th century and soon created a powerful empire. They developed a complex calendar and built vast cities of stone. Yet they had no iron tools, wheeled vehicles, or horses.

A mighty empire falls

Cortés entered the Aztec capital, Tenochtitlán, and took the emperor, Moctezuma II, hostage. Cortés was then forced to return to the coast to deal with charges of insubordination, and left the city in the charge of his lieutenant, Pedro de Alvarado. On his return, Cortés found that Alvarado had massacred a group of Aztec nobles. In response, the Aztecs revolted, killed Moctezuma, and forced the Spanish to flee. A year later, Cortés seized Tenochtitlán and took control of the entire Aztec Empire.

Time Line

November 18, 1518
Cortés leads an expedition from Cuba with 900 men

August 16, 1519
Cortés moves inland

November 1519
Cortés enters Tenochtitlán and takes the Aztec emperor, Moctezuma II, hostage

December 1519
The Aztecs revolt when Cortés is out of the city

June 30–July 1, 1520
Cortés fights his way out of Tenochtitlán, losing half his men

May–August 1521
The Spanish and their allies attack and seize Tenochtitlán

The city of Tenochtitlán, built on an island in Lake Texcoco.

Moctezuma II

The Aztec emperor Moctezuma II (reigned 1502–20) was portrayed as a weak leader in Spanish accounts. Before losing to Cortés, however, he had many military successes and conquered large parts of southern Mexico.

It's Amazing!

Tenochtitlán was not the first important city in the Valley of Mexico. The great city of Teotihuacán stood nearby many centuries earlier. The huge, sprawling Mexico City stands there today.

In search of the Incas

Rumors circulated in the New World of a gold-rich civilization known as Birù (or Peru) on the Pacific coast of South America. One man set out to look for this legendary civilization.

Head for the hills

Spanish explorer Francisco Pizarro led three expeditions to find Birù. The first found nothing. The second, in 1526, sailed as far south as the Inca city of Tumbes in northern Peru. It returned with news of an advanced civilization up in the mountains. Pizarro set out in 1530 to conquer it.

Francisco Pizarro

Pizarro (c.1475–1541) served as a soldier with Balboa in 1513 before becoming a cattle breeder in Panama. When he set out to conquer the Inca Empire in 1530, he was about 55. This was his last chance of glory.

The Inca Empire

The Inca Empire stretched the length of South America from Ecuador in the north to central Chile in the south and across the Andes to Argentina in the east. The empire was connected by a vast network of paved roads.

An Inca headdress, one of many objects the Incas made from gold.

Third time lucky

Pizarro and his party made their way south to Tumbes, which they now found in ruins following a civil war in the Inca Empire. With fewer than 200 men, Pizarro set out to meet the emperor, Atahuallpa. He took the emperor hostage and was offered a room full of gold and silver to release him. But when this treasure was handed over, Pizarro executed the emperor and seized the capital, Cusco. The Inca Empire was his.

Machu Picchu, a royal Inca retreat in the mountains of Peru, was abandoned by the Incas after the Spanish conquest and remained unknown to the outside world until 1911.

The ruins of Sacsahuamán.

Sacsahuamán fortress

This was the main Inca fortress guarding the capital, Cusco. It was a vast stone building with three massive terraced walls, capable of housing 5,000 soldiers. Inca stonemasons cut and shaped each stone individually.

Time Line

1524–25
Pizarro finds no gold on first voyage south

1526–28
Sails south to Tumbes, where he hears of a city in the mountains

May 1532
Returns to Tumbes, which he finds in ruins

November 1532
Heads inland to Cajamarca, where he takes Atahuallpa hostage

July 1533
Atahuallpa is executed

November 1533
Pizarro's army take the Inca capital Cusco

What Next?
The last Inca stronghold fell to the Spanish in 1572, but the edges of the empire remained largely unconquered until the early 1800s.

In search of gold

Spanish explorers obsessively searched for gold. They rarely found what they were looking for, and many lost their lives. They did, however, open up the interior of the continent for further exploration.

Time Line

May 1539
De Soto lands in Tampa Bay, Florida

1539–41
De Soto heads north and west, terrorizing the people he meets

February 1540
Coronado sets off in search of the mythical golden cities of Cibola

July 1540
Group dispatched by Coronado discovers the Grand Canyon

May 1541
De Soto crosses the Mississippi River

May 21, 1542
De Soto dies and his men return to New Spain (Mexico)

1542
Coronado returns to Mexico City

Conquering Florida

A decade after the disastrous expedition of 1528 (see page 117), Hernando de Soto took over responsibility for conquering Florida for Spain. His expedition took him through Florida and north to the Savannah River before heading west to the Mississippi River. De Soto inflicted great cruelty on the Cherokee, Cree, and other native people he met on his travels, but failed to find any gold.

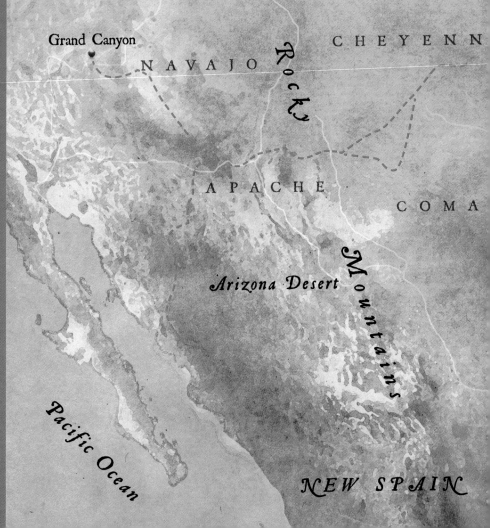

Grand Canyon

N A V A J O   Rocky   C H E Y E N N

A P A C H E   C O M A

Arizona Desert   Mountains

Pacific Ocean

NEW SPAIN

Chasing Cibola

On the western side of North America, another Spaniard went in search of gold, seeking the mythical city of Cibola. Francisco Vásquez de Coronado (c.1510–1554) headed an expedition north through what are now the states of New Mexico, Arizona, Texas, and Kansas. His men were the first Europeans to see the Grand Canyon.

The Arizona Desert

Vásquez de Coronado and his expedition crossed through the deserts of New Mexico and Arizona. Here, they encountered people, such as the Zuni and Hopi, who lived in huts built into the side of the cliffs. The climate was harsh, and many Spaniards lost their lives to Indian attacks.

A Kachina doll is a religious object made by the Hopi of the Arizona Desert.

N O R T H   A M E R I C A

OSAGE

VA

Mississippi River

CHEROKEE

Savannah River

E

FLORIDA

Tampa Bay

Gulf of Mexico

CUBA

-------- **Coronado Expedition (1540–42)**

-------- **De Soto Expedition (1539–42)**

Hernando de Soto

De Soto (c.1496–1542) was a Spanish nobleman who made his fortune conquering the Inca Empire with Pizarro. Now rich, he craved power, and in 1537 he was granted the right to conquer and colonize Florida.

Into Canada

While the Spanish explored Central America and Florida, the French concentrated on what is now Canada. They hoped to find a waterway through North America that would take them to Asia. What they discovered instead became the basis of a vast empire in the Americas.

First steps

In 1534, Jacques Cartier (1491–1557) set out to find a northwest passage to Asia. He sailed into the Gulf of St. Lawrence, and returned the following year and discovered the mighty St. Lawrence River—the gateway into Canada. Cartier sailed up the river, stopping at Stadacona (modern Québec) and Hochelaga. He named the hill near Hochelaga Mont Réal (Mount Royal), modern-day Montréal.

Woodland around the Great Lakes in dazzling fall splendor.

Sir Walter Raleigh

English adventurer Walter Raleigh (c.1552–1618) led an expedition in 1584 to set up an English colony in North America. The colony he founded at Roanoke in North Carolina lasted only a year.

It's a Mystery!

In 1587, 100 English settlers under Governor John White arrived on Roanoke Island. White returned to England for supplies, but when he came back in 1590 all the settlers had vanished without trace.

St. Lawrence River

Jacques Cartier found it impossible to sail up the St. Lawrence River and its tributaries because of the many white-water rapids above Montréal. Samuel de Champlain solved this problem by copying the locals and traveling by canoe.

The Hochelaga negotiated rapids in canoes.

French settlers

French fur trappers, traders, and fishermen followed Cartier to Canada, but it was not until the next century that an attempt was made to settle the area permanently. Samuel de Champlain (1567–1635) established Québec—one of the first French settlements in Canada. In 1615, he explored Lake Ontario.

Time Line

1534
Cartier explores the coast of Newfoundland

1535–36
Travels up St. Lawrence River to Montréal

1587
English colonists settle on Roanoke Island, but have all gone by 1590

1603
De Champlain explores the St. Lawrence up to Montréal

1608–9
Founds Québec

1615–16
Rows up Ottawa River by canoe, crosses overland to Lakes Ontario and Oneida

First nations

The French got on well with the native people, and used them as guides. De Champlain sided with the Algonquins, Hurons, and Montagnais against the Iroquois, who later helped the British throw the French out of Canada.

Chiefs of the Ottawa, who were allies of the French.

The mighty Mississippi

By the late 17th century, Europeans had successfully founded colonies in the south, east, and north of North America. But the interior of the continent remained relatively unknown to them. That changed after two extraordinary journeys by French explorers.

The new river

In 1673, fur trader Louis Jolliet (1645–1700), Jesuit priest Jacques Marquette (1637–75), and five others set out from the north to explore a great inland river they had heard about. They canoed down the Wisconsin River into the Mississippi, which they paddled down for more than 1,000 miles (1,600 km), until they met hostile Quapaw people and turned back. The Quapaw had Spanish goods, which suggested that the river emptied into the Gulf of Mexico, where the Spanish had set up colonies.

Cavelier de La Salle

René Robert Cavelier de La Salle (1643–87) was the son of a rich merchant from Rouen in France. He was training to become a priest before choosing a life of adventure and moving to the New World.

This print shows Jolliet and Marquette being paddled down the Mississippi by Illinois allies.

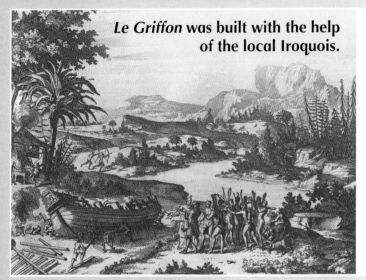
Le Griffon **was built with the help of the local Iroquois.**

Building *Le Griffon*

In 1678, La Salle built a ship, *Le Griffon*, at Niagara. It was the first full-size sailing ship on the Great Lakes. He built it to carry the furs he was hoping would pay for his expedition down the river. *Le Griffon* sailed through the Great Lakes and was soon laden with furs, but it sank on its way back to Niagara and the valuable cargo was lost.

What Next?

La Salle claimed the Mississippi basin for France, naming it Louisiana for the king, Louis XIV. This territory remained French until 1763. It was sold to the United States in 1803.

Time Line

May 17, 1673
Jolliet and Marquette cross Lake Michigan and paddle into Mississippi

July 17, 1673
The expedition meets Quapaw people and turns back near the Arkansas River

1678
La Salle sets up headquarters at Niagara on the Great Lakes

December 21, 1681
La Salle sets off for the Mississippi

April 6, 1682
La Salle reaches the delta; the party splits into three and meets three days later in the Gulf of Mexico

All the way down

In 1681, La Salle set off to explore the Mississippi River. Approaching the Mississippi via the Illinois River, the expedition canoed south until they, too, met the Quapaw near the Arkansas River. This time, the Quapaw allowed the party to continue south. In April 1682, the expedition reached the Mississippi Delta and the sea. The center of North America was now open to exploration and colonial settlement.

Mississippi Delta

When La Salle's expedition reached the delta at the mouth of the Mississippi, they split up to explore the vast marshes. The city of New Orleans was founded in 1718 to take advantage of the area's natural resources.

The Mississippi Delta seen from space.

Searching for the Western Sea

The first Spanish, French, and English explorers of North America had no idea just how big the continent was. Many believed that there was a sea in the interior that led to the Pacific Ocean. One man set out to find it.

The westward river

Pierre de Charlevoix arrived in Québec in 1720 and departed on his journey the next year. As he paddled through the Great Lakes he asked about the fabled Western Sea. French fur trappers could tell him nothing, while the locals just told him what he wanted to hear. But he did learn of "a great river that flows westward and empties into the southern sea."

De Charlevoix

Pierre François Xavier de Charlevoix (1682–1761) was a French Jesuit priest of noble birth, who first visited the New World in 1705. He returned in 1720 to investigate the Western Sea.

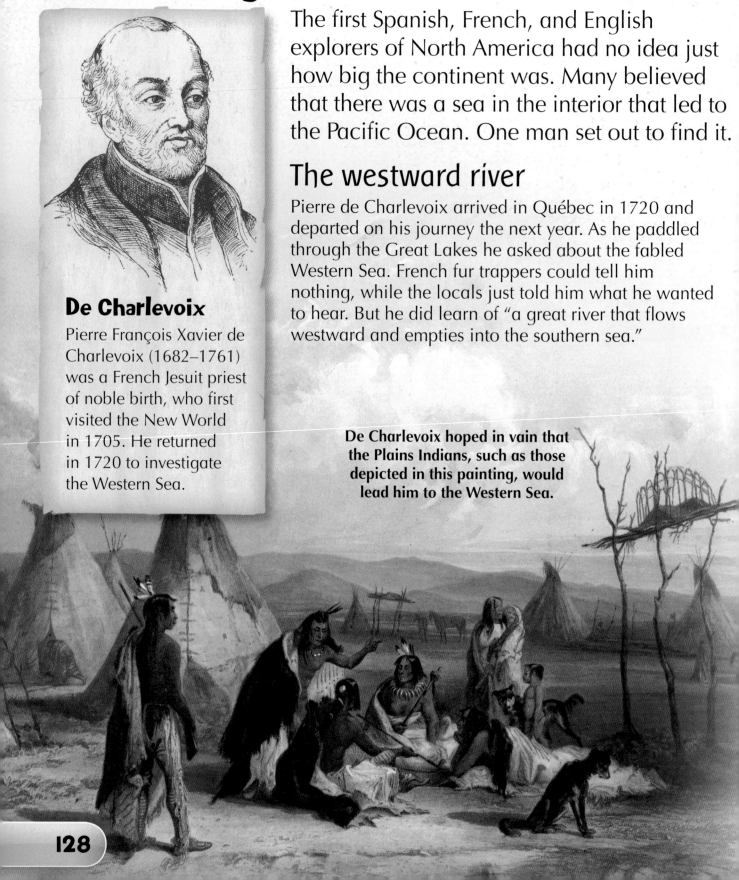

De Charlevoix hoped in vain that the Plains Indians, such as those depicted in this painting, would lead him to the Western Sea.

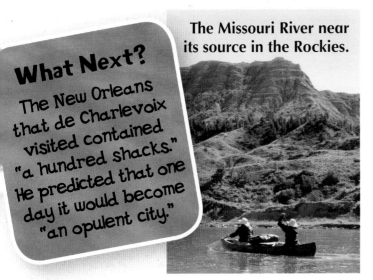

The Missouri River near its source in the Rockies.

What Next?
The New Orleans that de Charlevoix visited contained "a hundred shacks." He predicted that one day it would become "an opulent city."

The Missouri River

The Missouri River starts in the Rocky Mountains in southwest Montana. It then flows east and south for 2,340 miles (3,767 km) before joining the Mississippi at St. Louis. Its source is close to sources of rivers that flow west into the Columbia River and on into the Pacific Ocean. De Charlevoix guessed correctly that rivers would flow down the west side of the Rockies as well as the east.

The fruitless search

De Charlevoix set off in July 1721, retracing La Salle's route (see page 127) down the Mississippi to New Orleans. He found no Western Sea, because none exists, but he became convinced that any westward-flowing river would be found near the headwaters of the Missouri River. This prediction was later confirmed—but not for another 80 years.

Befriending the Sioux

De Charlevoix guessed that there were people west of the Sioux nation living near the Western Sea. He suggested that the French government should befriend the Sioux. French traders had already formed alliances with them, but a century and a half later, the Sioux would come into bloody conflict with settlers.

Sitting Bull, a 19th-century Sioux chief who fought the U.S. army.

Time Line

September 23, 1720
De Charlevoix arrives in Québec; after winter, paddles through the Great Lakes, mapping their shores

July 29, 1721
Sets off down the east side of Lake Michigan and into the St. Joseph River

September 1721
Stops for a month at Fort St. Joseph, where he studies the Miami peoples

December 1721
Spends Christmas at Natchez on the banks of the Mississippi

January 10, 1722
Arrives in New Orleans

The new frontier

In 1803, President Thomas Jefferson bought territory west of the Mississippi River from the French for $15 million. Jefferson commissioned an expedition to find out exactly what it was he had bought.

Heading west

The expedition was led by Jefferson's secretary, Meriwether Lewis, and his friend, William Clark. They were told to explore the newly acquired territory and to find a route through it to the Pacific coast. In May 1804, the pair set off from St. Louis on the banks of the Mississippi and canoed up the Missouri River toward the Rocky Mountains.

Time Line

May 14, 1804
Lewis and Clark leave St. Louis via the Missouri

October 1804
Expedition winters with the Mandan in North Dakota

April 9, 1805
Expedition sets off west

September 1805
They cross the Rockies

November 8, 1805
Reach the Pacific, building Fort Clatsop to spend the winter

March 1806
Expedition retraces its steps and canoes back down the Missouri

September 23, 1806
Expedition returns to St. Louis in triumph

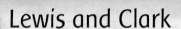

Lewis and Clark

Meriwether Lewis (1774–1809), pictured left, and William Clark (1770–1838), right, met while they were serving in the army. In 1803, Lewis asked Clark to become coleader of the Corps of Discovery, as the expedition was known. The pair worked very well with each other. Lewis was very good at organization, while Clark had vast experience in survival techniques and was a skilled mapmaker. They shared leadership duties, but Clark was the main guide through the dangerous Rockies.

Unlike other Plains Indians, the Mandan lived in permanent villages, such as this one, where the men are performing a bull dance.

Friendly locals

Lewis and Clark spent their first winter with the Mandan, a friendly tribe of hunters and farmers. While there, they were approached by a Montréal fur trapper, Toussaint Charbonneau, who wished to join the expedition. His wife Sacajawea was a Shoshone Indian. She proved invaluable as an interpreter and helped the expedition through potentially hostile territory.

It's Amazing!

In August 1805, the expedition made first contact with the Shoshone tribe. Their Shoshone guide, Sacajawea, took them to meet the tribe, and recognized its chief as her long-lost brother.

Crossing the Rockies

The expedition rode on horseback through the Rockies. They then paddled down toward the Columbia River. They reached the Pacific coast in November 1805. The route they had found to the Pacific was not easy. During their journey, however, they had made friendly contact with many tribes and found out a lot about this vast territory.

The Rocky Mountains lay across the route to the Pacific Ocean, and were very difficult to cross.

Hostile territory

The expedition faced many challenges while crossing the Rockies. Grizzly bears constantly attacked them, at one point chasing six men into the river. On another occasion a buffalo charged straight through their camp.

Grizzly bears are a constant threat in the Rockies.

Opening up the west

In the early 1840s, United States territory did not reach as far west as the Pacific Ocean. California was held by Mexico and Oregon was run jointly with Britain. The U.S. government settled these regions, hoping eventually to claim them as its own.

What Next?

The first pioneers set out along the newly mapped Oregon Trail in 1843. By 1845, at least 5,000 a year were making the journey.

The Oregon Trail

Explorer John Frémont opened up the west to potential settlers. On his first expedition in 1842, he surveyed the route from the Mississippi west to the South Pass, a 20-mile (32-km)-wide passage through the Rockies. The next year, he carried on through the pass and opened up the Oregon Trail to the Columbia River and the coast.

Pioneers on the Oregon Trail traveled in trains of about 10 wagons.

Frémont carried this flag on all his expeditions. The eagle is holding a pipe as a sign of friendship to the Indians.

Carrying the flag

John Frémont (1813–90) was the son of a French school teacher. From 1838, he surveyed new territories for the U.S. Army Topographical Corps. He subsequently made a fortune during the California Gold Rush of 1848, but lost all his money and died in poverty.

Kit Carson

Kit Carson (1809–68) was a fur trapper from Boone's Lick, Missouri, hired by Frémont as a guide to the Rocky Mountains. Frémont described Carson as the finest mountain man he had ever met. Carson worked with Frémont on all his expeditions.

The California Trail

In 1845, Frémont set out again, and opened up a trail via the Great Salt Lake to Sacramento in California. After a war with Mexico, California and other Mexican areas were taken by the United States by 1847. By then, the British had already given up all claims on Oregon. The territory of the United States now reached the Pacific coast, and settlers began to travel there along the routes pioneered by Frémont.

Time Line

1842
Frémont surveys a route from the Mississippi to the South Pass

1843–44
On his second journey, Frémont opens up the Oregon Trail, then travels to southern California and treks east through Sierra Nevada

March 1845
Frémont surveys California Trail to Sacramento

March 1846
Frémont raises U.S. flag in California

1848
Treaty of Guadalupe–Hidalgo gives United States control of Utah, California, Nevada, and parts of Arizona and New Mexico

The Great Salt Lake

On September 6, 1843, Frémont and his team saw the Great Salt Lake, describing the area as suitable for settlement. This attracted Brigham Young's Christian sect, the Mormons, to the area, although Young later described it as a desert.

The water in the Great Salt Lake is even saltier than sea water.

Scientific explorers

After explorers had discovered new lands, scientists set out to find out about the strange new plants and wildlife there. Their discoveries, most notably in the rich environment of the Amazon rain forest, have led to great advances in scientific knowledge.

South American studies

French scientist Charles-Marie de la Condamine (1701–74) sailed to Ecuador in 1735. He wanted to measure the size and shape of the world—a science known as geodesy. He stayed to study the area's plants and animals. In the early 1800s, German Alexander von Humboldt and Frenchman Aimé Bonpland (1773–1858) explored the Andes, recording 3,000 new plant species.

Alexander von Humboldt

Humboldt (1769–1859) explored the Orinoco River in Venezuela, and then traveled down the Andes from the Caribbean to Peru. He made important discoveries in many scientific fields and was described by Charles Darwin as "the greatest scientific traveler who ever lived."

Drawings by Bates of some of the butterflies he found in Amazonia.

The collector

Henry Bates (1825–92) was an English clerk with an avid interest in botany. After 11 years in South America, he returned to Great Britain with about 14,000 insect and butterfly specimens. At least half of them were unknown to European scientists at the time.

The great age

The 19th century was the great age of scientific exploration. Henry Bates, Alfred Wallace (1823–1913), and Richard Spruce (1817–93) all spent years in the Amazon, collecting animal and plant specimens. Charles Darwin (1809–82) visited the offshore Galápagos Islands in 1835. His observations of the islands' extraordinary wildlife led him to develop his ideas about how species develop, known as the theory of evolution.

The Amazon rain forest, one of the richest natural environments in the world, is where thousands or even millions of species are yet to be discovered.

What Next?

After four years in the Amazon rain forest, Alfred Wallace set sail for home in 1852. Sadly, his ship caught fire off Bermuda and he lost all his specimens and notes.

Time Line

1735–44
La Condamine studies wildlife in Ecuador

1799–1804
Humboldt and Bonpland explore the River Orinoco and the Andes

1832–35
Darwin sails around South America and the Galápagos Islands on board the *Beagle*

1848–52
Wallace collects thousands of specimens but loses them to a fire

1849–64
Spruce collects plant specimens in Amazonia

1850–59
Bates collects insect specimens in Amazonia

Modern discoveries

Scientists are discovering more species of animal and plant than ever. Nearly 2 million have been described, but there may be as many as 50 million left to discover. In the last 20 years alone, nearly 2,000 new species of amphibian have been found.

New species of amphibian, such as this South American tree frog, are discovered every year.

Darwin in the Galápagos

Charles Darwin studied medicine and then for the priesthood, giving up on both ideas. With nothing else to do, he took the post of naturalist onboard the Beagle, a survey ship bound for South America. This is an extract from his account of his visit to the Galápagos Islands off the coast of Chile—a visit that was to help him form his revolutionary theory of the evolution of the species.

The different finches of the islands have beaks of many shapes and sizes, depending on their feeding habits.

September 17, 1835

The Bay swarmed with animals. Fish, sharks, and turtles popped their heads up all around. These islands are paradises for all sorts of reptiles. There are three kinds of turtle, and there are so many tortoises that a single ship's company caught over 500 in a very short time. The little birds are very trusting, and hopped about within three or four feet of us.

September 21

In my walk I met two very large tortoises (circumference of shell about 7 ft). One ate a cactus and then quietly walked away. The other gave a deep and loud hiss and drew back his head. They were so heavy I could barely lift them off the ground. Surrounded by the black lava, the leafless shrubs, and large cacti, they look like old-fashioned, ancient animals; or rather inhabitants of some other planet.

Galápagos Islands

Santiago

Baltra

Rabida

San Cristobal

Fernandina

Santa Fe

Isabela

Santa Cruz

Floreana

Española

September 25

Mr. Lawson remembers seeing a terrapin that six men could scarcely lift and two could not turn over on its back. These immense creatures must be very old. In the year 1830, one was caught by whalers. It had various dates carved on its shell, and one was 1786. The only reason it was not carried away there and then must have been that it was too big for two men to manage. The whalers always send off their men in pairs to hunt.

September 27

I collected all the animals, plants, insects, and reptiles from this island. I will compare these specimens with creatures from elsewhere. In this way, I shall work out to which district or center of creation the organized beings of these islands must be attached.

THE PACIFIC AND AUSTRALIA

Although European explorers had crossed the Pacific Ocean by the 16th century, most of this vast body of water was still known to only Polynesian travelers. Europeans believed that the Pacific bordered a vast southern continent, but nobody was sure where it was. Expeditions set sail to discover this "new" continent. During their travels, European navigators mapped the ocean, explored its islands, and found a smaller continent.

The incredible Polynesians

Long before Europeans arrived in the Pacific Ocean, navigators had already explored the ocean and colonized its many islands. Their perilous voyages are among the most remarkable human expeditions of all time.

A Polynesian double canoe, similar in design to a modern-day catamaran.

Who were they?

The first inhabitants of the Pacific islands moved east from Indonesia in around 2000 B.C., reaching Fiji, Tonga, and Samoa by 1000 B.C. Here, they developed a distinctive Polynesian culture. In about 200 B.C., they began to seek new islands, sailing east to Tahiti and Easter Island, north to Hawaii, then south to Aotearoa (New Zealand).

The Maori

Aotearoa was the last island group to be colonized. The Maori, as the new settlers were known, adapted their customs to live off the islands' unique animals and plants.

It's Amazing!

When Captain Cook measured a Maori canoe in Aotearoa in 1770, he found it was longer than the ship he was sailing.

A Maori man with traditional facial tattoos.

Time Line

c.2000 B.C.
Austronesian people from Indonesia spread to New Guinea

c.1000 B.C.
Lapita people reach Fiji, Tonga, and Samoa

c.200 B.C.
Polynesians sail east to Tahiti and on to Marquesas Islands

c. A.D. 300
Polynesians reach Easter Island

c. A.D. 400
Polynesians sail north to Line Islands and Hawaii

c. A.D. 1000
Polynesians colonize Aotearoa (New Zealand)

More than 800 of these giant statues stand on Easter Island. Nobody knows why they were made.

Easter Island

Easter Island is more than 1,000 miles (1,600 km) from its nearest island neighbor and is so remote that the islanders believed they were the only people on the Earth. They were the only Polynesians to develop a form of writing.

Navigation techniques

The Polynesians had no instruments to guide them. Instead, they navigated by observing changes in the wind and currents, looking at wave patterns, and following migrating birds. They also used the sun and stars. Each island had its "on top" star, so that when, for example, Sirius was overhead, they knew they were in the same latitude as Tahiti. Using these simple methods, they colonized the entire Pacific Ocean.

Stick charts

Polynesian navigators were trained using a stick chart, such as this one from the Marshall Islands. The charts were made of a network of palm sticks tied together with coconut fiber. Shells threaded onto the sticks marked the position of each island relative to the ocean currents, allowing a navigator to learn the geography of the region.

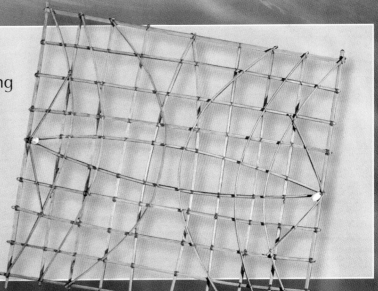

Into the southern seas

In the 16th century, following Magellan's lead, a number of Spanish and Portuguese explorers set out across the Pacific, discovering new islands and attempting to colonize the region with European settlers.

Solomon Islands

Mendaña explored many of the Solomon Islands. Conflict broke out with the inhabitants when the Spanish went in search of food.

A mask (right) and paddle (above) from the Solomon Islands.

Failed settlers

In 1567, Alvaro de Mendaña (1541–95) sailed west from Peru, intending to convert people to Christianity and set up a Spanish settlement. He discovered the Solomon Islands, but it was a disastrous voyage. His ship was almost destroyed in a hurricane, forcing the crew to make sails out of blankets. Most of the crew died before they could reach safety. Almost 30 years later, Mendaña died in a failed attempt to settle the Solomons.

Another try

In 1605, Pedro Fernández de Quirós (1565–1614) set out to discover the southern continent. He visited the Cook Islands and Vanuatu, but then abandoned the expedition. Luis Váez de Torres (c.1565–1613) took over the expedition and sailed around New Guinea.

Forgotten lands

After Mendaña left the Solomons in 1568, the islands were completely forgotten until 1767. Torres's voyage around New Guinea in 1607 was not properly recognized until 1762.

Fishermen on the Solomon islands.

Men from New Guinea perform a ceremonial dance.

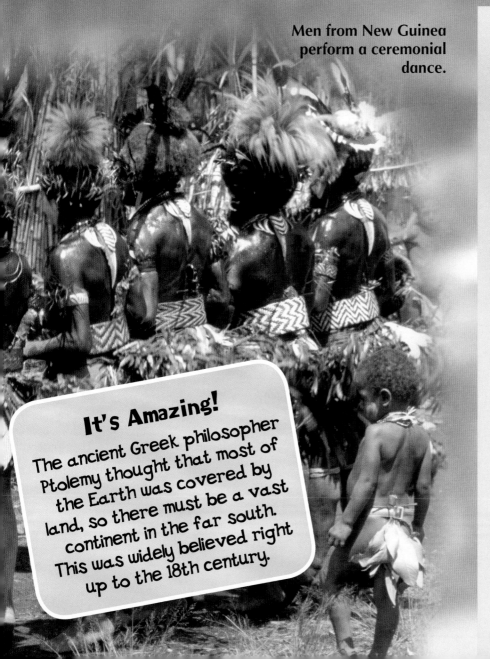

It's Amazing!

The ancient Greek philosopher Ptolemy thought that most of the Earth was covered by land, so there must be a vast continent in the far south. This was widely believed right up to the 18th century.

Time Line

February 1568
Mendaña discovers Solomon Islands

August 15, 1568
Two ships sail for home but are separated; Mendaña lands in America in November

April 1595
Sets out again for the Solomons, but dies in the Santa Cruz islands

December 21, 1605
Quirós searches for the southern continent

May 1606
Quirós reaches Vanuatu, then sails for home; Torres takes over

May 1607
Torres sails between New Guinea and Australia

Around Australia

In two epic voyages, the Dutch explorer Abel Tasman sailed around Australia and explored its northern coast. Despite proving that this new continent was not part of a larger southern continent, his expeditions were considered a failure.

What Next?
The Dutch never publicized Tasman's voyages, because they did not want anyone else to know about the newly discovered lands in the Pacific.

New Guinea

Batavia

Torres Strait

Pacific Ocean

→ **First expedition (1642–43)**

← **Second expedition (1644)**

Australia

Abel Tasman

Abel Tasman (1603–59) was born in Lutjegast, Holland. In 1634, he moved to Batavia (now Jakarta) on Java, where he was employed as a captain by the Dutch East India Company. After his voyages, he became a judge in Batavia.

Van Diemen's Land

South of the continent

In 1642, Tasman sailed west from Batavia across the Indian Ocean to Mauritius. His mission was to explore the land south of Java and find a passage between the Indian and Pacific oceans to lead Dutch sailors to the riches of South America. From Mauritius, Tasman sailed south and east, becoming the first European to visit Tasmania (which he named Van Diemen's Land), New Zealand, and Fiji. The voyage took him all the way around Australia, and proved conclusively that it was not the fabled "Great South Land."

Exploration

For his second voyage, Tasman attempted to establish the relationships of New Guinea, Australia, the new Van Diemen's Land, and the "unknown South Land" (Antarctica). However, he failed to recognize the Torres Strait, and returned to Batavia after sailing along Australia's north coast.

Tasman Sea

New Zealand

N

NW

W

SW

S

Time Line

August 14, 1642
Tasman sets sail from Batavia to find a short cut to Chile and explore the "Great South Land"

December 13, 1642
Sights South Island of New Zealand, which he believes to be part of the southern continent; mistakes strait between the islands for a bay

April 1643
Discovers Fiji

February 29, 1644
Sets sail for New Guinea and Australia via the Torres Strait, which he mistakes for a bay; explores north coast of Australia then returns to Batavia

Dutch East Indies

The Dutch East India Company was set up in 1602 to challenge Spanish and Portuguese control of the spice trade. Basing itself in Batavia, its large fleet of ships quickly gained control of many of the seas around southeast Asia.

A 17th-century painting of the Dutch East India Company's private fleet.

The first voyage of Captain Cook

Despite many voyages across the Pacific, the ocean remained largely unknown to Europeans well into the 18th century. So the quest for the great southern continent remained as intense as ever.

Circling New Zealand

In 1768, the Royal Society, a body set up in Great Britain to promote science, asked James Cook to supervise an expedition to Tahiti. They wanted him to observe the path of the planet Venus across the sun. The British Admiralty supported the expedition, hoping to discover the great southern continent. Cook arrived in the south Pacific in April 1769 and sailed around both islands of New Zealand, proving they were not part of a larger continent.

Time Line

August 26, 1768
Cook leaves Plymouth; collects plant specimens on Tierra del Fuego

April 13, 1769
Anchors off Tahiti for three months

October 1769
Reaches New Zealand and sails around the two islands

April 29, 1770
Lands at Botany Bay

October 1770
Sails up west coast of Australia, around northern tip, and reaches Batavia via the Torres Strait

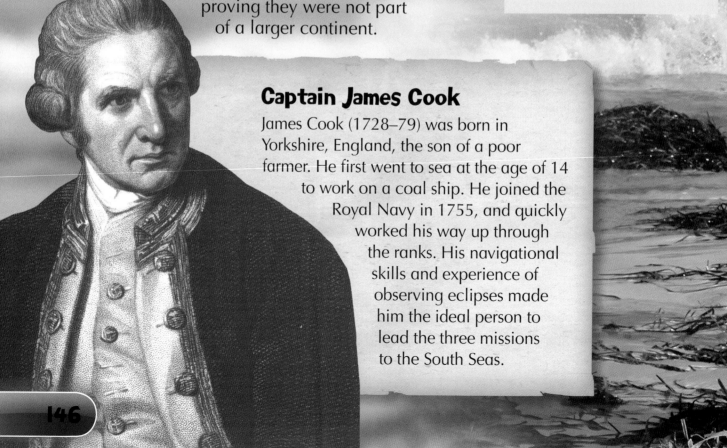

Captain James Cook

James Cook (1728–79) was born in Yorkshire, England, the son of a poor farmer. He first went to sea at the age of 14 to work on a coal ship. He joined the Royal Navy in 1755, and quickly worked his way up through the ranks. His navigational skills and experience of observing eclipses made him the ideal person to lead the three missions to the South Seas.

The *Endeavour*

The *Endeavour* was a converted coal ship similar to the ones Cook sailed in when he first went to sea. The ship was not elegant or fast but it was large. It was roomy enough to accommodate a crew of 94 men plus their stores, and tough enough for the long voyage.

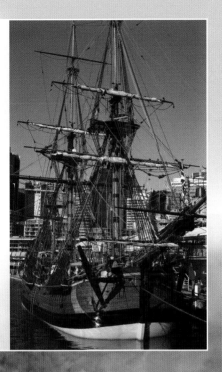

A replica of the *Endeavour* in Whitby, Yorkshire.

First landing

Cook sailed west across the Tasman Sea, sighting land on the southeast coast of Australia at Point Hicks on April 19. Ten days later he landed at Botany Bay. Continuing northward, Cook ran aground on the Great Barrier Reef and was forced to land to make repairs. He then sailed to Batavia via the Torres Strait before returning home.

It's Amazing!

When Cook's crew first saw a kangaroo, they were unsure what type of animal it was. The size of a deer, but jumping like a hare, they decided it must be a "kind of stag."

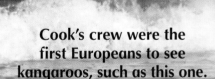

Cook's crew were the first Europeans to see kangaroos, such as this one.

New discoveries

Naturalists Joseph Banks and Daniel Solander were onboard the *Endeavour*, along with painter Sydney Parkinson. Together, they recorded many new exotic plants, animals, and insects.

A drawing by Sydney Parkinson of red honeysuckle.

147

Discovering Antarctica

For his second expedition, Cook was sent on a final search for the legendary southern continent. The British Admiralty was still not sure whether the southern continent really existed.

Crossing the Circle

Cook sailed south down the Atlantic Ocean and continued south until he crossed the Antarctic Circle—he was the first explorer to do so. He then sailed through the Southern Ocean to New Zealand and took on more supplies before heading south again. The mythical continent was thought to lie somewhere between New Zealand and Cape Horn.

What next?

After his second voyage, Cook wrote a report on how to prevent scurvy, a potentially fatal disease caused by a lack of vitamin C.

Time Line

July 13, 1772
Cook sets sail with two ships in search of the southern continent

January 17, 1773
Crosses Antarctic Circle and sails to New Zealand for supplies

November 1774
Sailing south to Antarctica, Cook's two ships are separated; the *Adventure* returns to England

December 1774
The *Resolution* is surrounded by icebergs

July 29, 1775
Having survived the winter, Cook returns home via Cape Horn

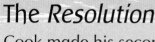

A drawing from 1809 of the *Resolution* surrounded by packed ice off Antarctica.

The *Resolution*

Cook made his second voyage with the *Resolution* and the *Adventure*. They were both converted coal ships, whose strong hulls protected them from icebergs. The *Resolution* was originally named the *Drake*, after explorer and pirate Sir Francis Drake, but this was changed to avoid upsetting the Spanish.

Cook attends a village meeting on Tahiti.

Tahiti

On each of his voyages, Cook stopped off in Tahiti. When he saw that Tahitians and Easter Islanders could understand each other, he began to suspect that South Sea islanders all shared a common ancestry.

The southern continent

Finding only a few small islands, Cook returned to New Zealand before sailing south again. He crossed the Antarctic Circle twice more before icebergs forced him north. Having sailed right around the South Pole, he could rule out the existence of a massive continent. However, he believed that he had found a large piece of land near the Pole.

The coastline of Antarctica, which Cook believed he saw.

Sea chronometer

Until Cook's time, navigators had been able to calculate latitude (position north–south) but not longitude (east–west). In 1760, James Harrison developed the chronometer for accurately measuring longitude. Cook used this on his second voyage.

The H5, one of Harrison's chronometers.

Cook's final voyage

On his final voyage, Cook set out to find the northwest passage between the Atlantic and Pacific oceans. Two other expeditions searched for a passage from the Atlantic side, while Cook looked for one from the Pacific.

It's Amazing!

Among the crew of the Resolution was William Bligh. Years later, in 1787, he was made captain of HMS Bounty. His crew mutinied and set Bligh and 18 others adrift in a small boat.

Finding Hawaii

Setting sail with both the *Resolution* and the *Discovery*, Cook left England in July 1776. He sailed south to Cape Town and then across the Indian Ocean to New Zealand. He revisited Tahiti, and what are now known as the Cook Islands. He then sailed north, finding the previously unknown volcanic Hawaiian Islands, which he named the Sandwich Isles.

The NuuChahNulth

As Cook sailed up the American coast, he missed the strait between Vancouver Island and the mainland, and anchored in Nootka Sound. Here, the local NuuChahNulth people greeted him wearing elaborate masks and painted faces.

A NuuChahNulth totem pole carved from a cedar tree.

Time Line

July 12, 1776
Cook sets sail from Plymouth

January 1777
Heads to New Zealand and on to Tahiti and the Cook Islands

December 1777
Lands on an island he calls Christmas Island

January 1778
Reaches Hawaii, then cruises up the North American coastline

August 18, 1778
Becomes icebound in the Arctic Ocean and heads south again

January 17, 1779
Returns to Hawaii

February 14, 1779
Cook is killed on Hawaii Island

The Aleutian Islands

The Aleutian Islands stretch from southwest Alaska along the south of the Bering Sea. Vitus Bering was the first to explore the islands in 1741 (see pages 50–51). Cook sailed along the eastern end of the chain before he headed north into the Bering Sea.

Cook's final days

In spring and summer 1778, Cook explored the North American coast from Oregon north to Alaska. He sailed down the Aleutian Islands before turning north again into the Bering Sea. He became increasingly unsure that he would find the passage. When ice surrounded his ships, he headed back to Hawaii, where he was killed on February 14, 1779.

Mauna Kea is the largest of five volcanoes on Hawaii Island.

The Death of Cook

Cook tried to deal fairly with the people he met. In Hawaii, however, the islanders stole one of his small boats. Cook planned to take the local king hostage to get his boat back. As Cook negotiated, his crew opened fire and the islanders stabbed Cook to death.

Knives are drawn as Cook's men open fire.

Cook lands in Australia

Captain James Cook first caught sight of the southeast tip of Australia on April 19, 1770. He then sailed northeast up the coast. Sailing with him were Tupia, a native of Tahiti, and two naturalists, Joseph Banks and Daniel Solander. This is his account of landing at Botany Bay.

Saturday, April 28

We are now less than two miles from the shore, so Mr. Banks, Dr. Solander, Tupia, and I set off toward land in a small boat. Four or five natives took to the woods as we approached the shore. To our disappointment, we could find no safe place to land.

In the morning, we found a bay that was quite well sheltered from the wind. I decided to sail the ship into this bay, and sent the master ahead to see how we could enter it.

Sunday, April 29

As we sailed by, we saw several natives on both sides of the bay. There were a few huts, men, women, and children on the south shore, and I approached by rowing boat, hoping to speak with them. As we came near, they all took off, except two men who seemed resolved to oppose our landing. When I saw this, I immediately ordered the oarsmen to stop rowing so that I could speak to the two men. But neither Tupia nor any other of my men could understand one word they said. Shortly after this we landed and, as soon as we did so, they threw two darts at us.

Sunday, May 6

In the evening, the small sailing yawl returned from a fishing expedition. They caught two stingrays weighing near 600 pounds. I have given this place the name of Botany Bay, in honor of the large quantity of new plants that Mr. Banks and Dr. Solander have collected here.

The tragic voyage of La Pérouse

Captain Cook's voyages did much to map the Pacific Ocean and clear up any confusion about the southern continent. But the French government wanted to know more, and in 1785 sent a naval expedition to the ocean. It was led by Comte de La Pérouse.

The mission

La Pérouse's mission was to fill any gaps in the knowledge of the Pacific Ocean left by Cook. La Pérouse set sail from France with two ships. After rounding Cape Horn, he cruised up the eastern Pacific to Alaska, but failed to find any northwest passage. He then headed across the ocean to China.

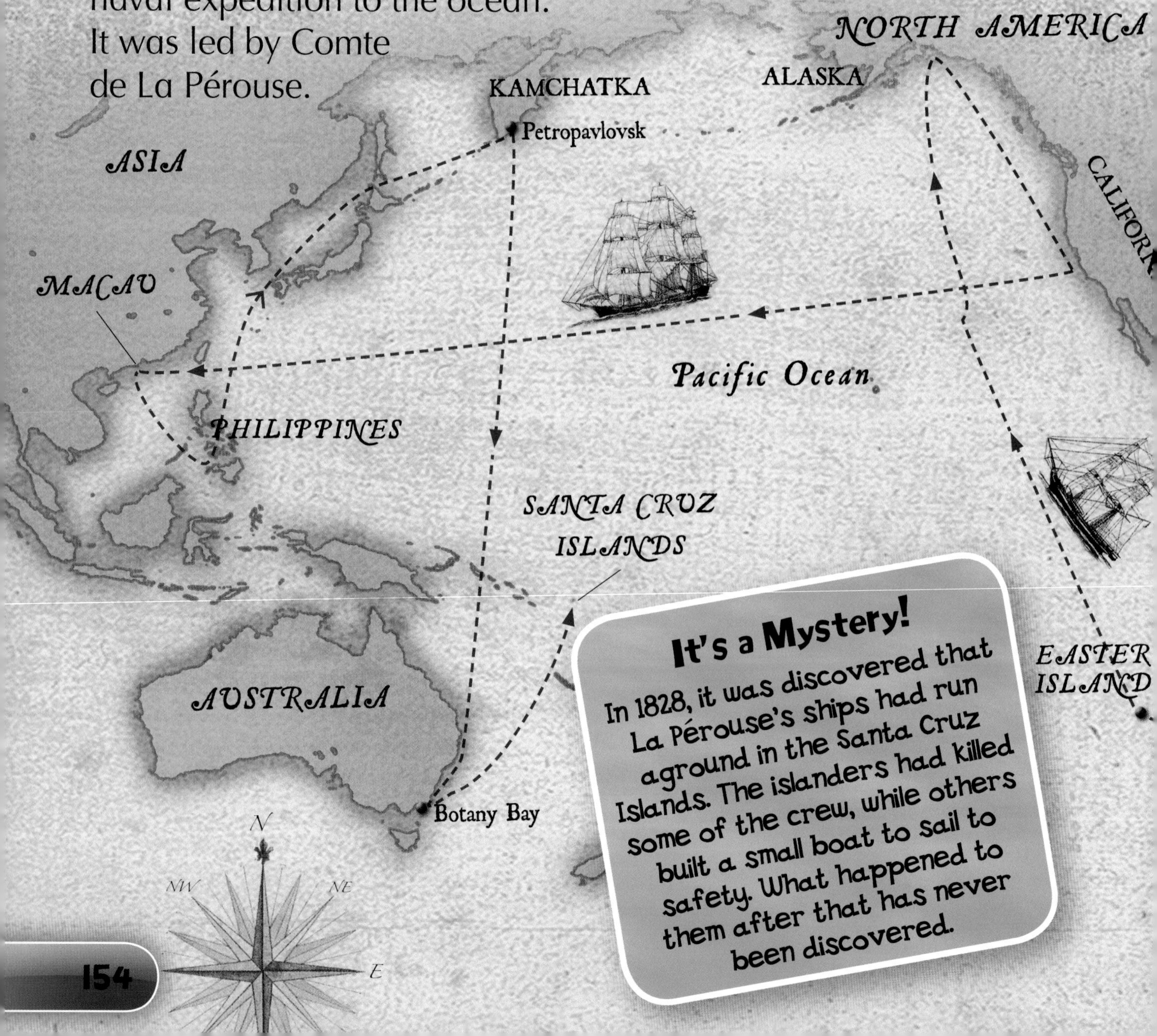

NORTH AMERICA

ALASKA

CALIFORNIA

KAMCHATKA

Petropavlovsk

ASIA

MACAU

Pacific Ocean

PHILIPPINES

SANTA CRUZ ISLANDS

EASTER ISLAND

AUSTRALIA

Botany Bay

N

NW

NE

E

It's a Mystery!

In 1828, it was discovered that La Pérouse's ships had run aground in the Santa Cruz Islands. The islanders had killed some of the crew, while others built a small boat to sail to safety. What happened to them after that has never been discovered.

Time Line

August 1, 1785
La Pérouse leaves France with the *Boussole* and the *Astrolabe*

April 1786
Enters the Pacific and heads north

September 24, 1786
Leaves California and sails west

September 1787
Reaches Petropavlovsk in Kamchatka, where he receives orders to sail to Australia

January 24, 1788
Sails into Botany Bay

March 10, 1788
Sails north and is never seen again

1828
French explorers find wrecks of the two ships on Santa Cruz Islands

Comte de La Pérouse

Jean-François de Galaup, Comte (Count) de La Pérouse (1741–88), was a French nobleman who joined the navy at the age of 15. By the 1780s, he had commanded several ships, making him the ideal candidate for the expedition of 1785.

EUROPE

FRANCE

AFRICA

Lost at sea

La Pérouse sailed north to the Kamchatka Peninsula in Siberia, where a letter from France ordered him to investigate a settlement in New South Wales, Australia. He reached Botany Bay just after the British had set up a prison colony there. He headed north again toward New Guinea, but neither he nor his crew were ever seen again.

SOUTH AMERICA

Valparaiso

Cape Horn

La Pérouse's legacy

From the various places he landed, La Pérouse took the opportunity to send back to Europe the logs, papers, paintings, and charts made during his voyage. These were published in an atlas in 1798.

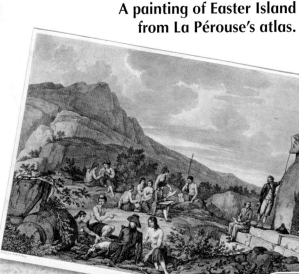

A painting of Easter Island from La Pérouse's atlas.

Inland Australia

In 1788, the first British settlers arrived in Sydney Cove to set up a prison colony there. The coast of Australia was still little known and the vast interior totally unexplored.

Opening up the continent

From 1798–99, the English naval captain Matthew Flinders (1774–1814) and the surgeon George Bass (1771–1803) mapped much of the coastline south of Sydney. They also sailed around Tasmania, proving it was an island. Two years later, Flinders circled the whole continent. The interior of Australia remained a mystery until 1813, when a route was discovered through the Blue Mountains that lay behind Sydney.

Charles Sturt

Charles Sturt (1795–1869) was born in India, the son of a British judge. He was educated in England before going to Australia in 1826 as a soldier to guard convicts. He liked the country immediately and became one of its first inland explorers.

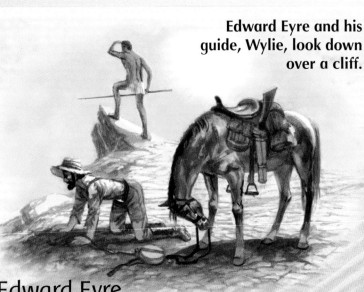

Edward Eyre and his guide, Wylie, look down over a cliff.

Edward Eyre

Englishman Edward Eyre (1815–1901) emigrated to Australia aged 17. He became the manager of a sheep station in South Australia, and explored the region in 1839. A year later, he set off across southern Australia in search of land for grazing.

It's Amazing!

Before 1824, the name "Australia" applied to the whole South Pacific region. The continent we know by this name today was called Terra Australis or New Holland.

Australian Aborigines

The aboriginal people walked across a land bridge (no longer there) from Asia to Australia about 40,000 years ago and slowly spread across the continent. They were nomadic hunters and gatherers who lived in small groups. Each group spoke its own language and had its own laws.

This boy is holding two boomerangs, Aboriginal tools for hunting.

The Simpson Desert in the center of Australia was visited by Charles Sturt in 1845.

Time Line

1788
First convicts and guards arrive at Sydney Cove

1798–99
Matthew Flinders and George Bass map the southwest coast

1801–3
Flinders sails around Australia

1829–30
Charles Sturt discovers the Darling River

1839–40
Edward Eyre explores inland South Australia

1841
Eyre crosses from Adelaide to Western Australia

1844–46
Sturt treks inland to the Simpson Desert

Into the interior

In two expeditions in 1828 and 1830, Charles Sturt mapped Australia's two major rivers, the Murray and Darling. This opened up what is now inland New South Wales to farmers and settlers. Sturt later ventured toward the center of Australia, looking for an inland sea, but only found desert. In 1841, Edward Eyre trekked from Adelaide in South Australia west along the arid coast of the Great Australian Bight to Albany at the southern tip of Western Australia. With not a single river along the route, Eyre was forced to dig deep wells in the sand, and would have died if it hadn't started to rain.

So close, yet so far!

Many people believed Australia was so vast it must contain an inland sea. In 1860, the South Australian government decided to find out. It offered a large cash prize to the first person to cross the continent from south to north.

Early setbacks

Robert Burke's expedition seemed well equipped. It set out from Melbourne with 18 men, 24 camels, 28 horses, and 21 tons (23 tonnes) of provisions. But when the camel master and the doctor quit at Menindee, 400 miles (640 km) north of Melbourne, Burke decided to leave most of his supplies behind and continue with a small group. At Cooper's Creek, he left William Brahe in charge of the remaining party, and set out north with William Wills, John King, Charles Gray, and provisions for 12 weeks.

The mudflats at the Gulf of Carpentaria.

Time Line

August 21, 1860
Burke's expedition sets out from Melbourne

October 19, 1860
Two men drop out at Menindee

December 16, 1860
Burke establishes supply depot at Cooper's Creek

February 9, 1861
Expedition reaches the tidal Flinders River but does not see the sea

April 21, 1861
Burke, Wills, and King return to find Cooper's Creek deserted

June 1861
Burke and Wills die of starvation; King is rescued by Aborigines

Burke and Wills

Robert O'Hara Burke (1821–61), left, was born in Ireland and emigrated to Australia, where he became a police officer in Melbourne. His expedition into the interior was his first experience of the Australian outback (remote dry areas). William John Wills (1834–61), right, became Burke's second in command when the camel master defected.

Beasts of burden

Camels are not native to Australia, but were introduced in the 1840s to carry goods in the outback. Some of them escaped—these were the ancestors of Australia's wild camel population.

Almost there

On February 9, 1861, Burke's party reached the tidal estuary of the Flinders River in the Gulf of Carpentaria. They never saw the coast because wide mudflats stood between them and the sea. Almost immediately they headed south again, with Gray dying of dysentery on the way. In April, they arrived at Cooper's Creek to find it deserted. Within two months, Burke and Wills had both died of starvation.

What Next?

Robert Burke was criticized for his poor handling of the expedition, but both he and Wills were later recognized for their bravery by a memorial in Melbourne.

Lost in the bush

When Burke and his two colleagues arrived back in Cooper's Creek, William Brahe had left just hours earlier. Wills and King wanted to try to catch up with him, but Burke insisted on heading for Mount Hopeless 150 miles (240 km) to the southwest. Their food ran out, and Burke and Wills died. King was rescued when he was found by Aborigines.

Burke, Wills, and King were lost in the bush. Only King survived.

McDouall Stuart

Scottish-born John McDouall Stuart (1815–66) moved to South Australia in 1838 to work as a surveyor. In 1844, he joined Charles Sturt's unsuccessful expedition to reach the center of the continent (see pages 156–157).

Winning the prize

The prize offered by the South Australian government to cross the continent from south to north proved irresistible to John Stuart. He was so determined to win he made three attempts in just two years!

Failed expedition

In March 1860, Stuart set out from Adelaide in South Australia with just two travel companions. A month later, he made it just over half way there, reaching Tenant Creek. Here, he had to turn back because Aborigines had set fire to the bush in front of him to defend their land.

The view from the summit of Central Mount Stuart.

The British flag is raised in triumph on the shores of the Indian Ocean.

Mount Stuart

On his first attempt to cross Australia, Stuart reached the exact center of the continent. He named a nearby hill Central Mount Sturt "after the father of Australian exploration." The hill was later renamed Central Mount Stuart after its discoverer.

Pride of Adelaide

The city of Adelaide was founded in 1836, when the British established a colony in South Australia. The city was anxious to make its mark on Australian history, so it offered the prize to cross the continent in 1860.

A statue of John McDouall Stuart in Adelaide.

Try and try again

On his second attempt in early 1861, with a far larger party of 13 men and 49 horses, Stuart came within 200 miles (320 km) of the sea, but turned back when a thicket of thorn bushes blocked his way. In October 1861, he tried again. This time he reached the north coast of Australia at Chambers Bay. The continent had been successfully crossed at last.

Time Line

March 2, 1860
Stuart and two companions leave Adelaide to cross Australia, but turn back half way

January 1, 1861
Stuart sets off again

September 1861
Returns to Adelaide 200 miles (320 km) short of the north coast

October 1861
Begins third attempt to cross Australia

July 1862
Reaches Indian Ocean

December 1862
Returns home, having lost the use of his limbs due to scurvy

What Next?

An overland telegraph line was opened along Stuart's route nine years later. From Darwin on the north coast, the line ran under the sea, connecting Australia to Indonesia and Asia.

A raft of discovery

Most explorers left home in search of adventure or wealth, or to discover new lands to settle. Very few set out to prove a personal theory that could revolutionize history. Thor Heyerdahl was one such explorer.

The new theory

The accepted view about the origins of the Polynesians is that their ancestors populated the Pacific islands from southeast Asia by around A.D. 1000 (see pages 140–141). However, Thor Heyerdahl was convinced that the Pacific islands had been colonized in two big migrations from the Americas in the east, the first by A.D. 500, and the second in about A.D. 1100.

Thor Heyerdahl

Norwegian explorer Thor Heyerdahl (1914–2002) became fascinated by Polynesia while at university. He lived for a year with his wife in the wild in Tahiti, but found the experience difficult to cope with.

Kon-Tiki, a raft 45 feet (13.7 m) long and 18 feet (5.5 m) wide.

Inca rafts

The Spanish forces who conquered the Inca Empire (see pages 120–121) made drawings of Inca rafts built to sail on Lake Titicaca. These formed the basis of *Kon-Tiki*'s design.

People around Lake Titicaca still make boats out of reeds, similar to the boats of the Incas.

A raft across the Pacific

Heyerdahl set out to prove his theory by building a balsawood and bamboo raft similar to those of the Incas. Named *Kon-Tiki* after a Polynesian god, the raft set out from Peru on a 101-day journey that took Heyerdahl and his crew 5,000 miles (8,000 km) across the Pacific to Raroia in the Tuamotu Islands in Tahiti. Heyerdahl had shown that the first Polynesians could have sailed from South America. However, there is no proof that they made such a journey.

Sweet potato

Most historians believe that early Polynesians probably sailed as far east as South America, because both the Maoris of New Zealand and the Polynesians of the eastern Pacific had cultivated the sweet potato, a native plant of that continent. Heyerdahl claimed that native South Americans had taken the sweet potato with them on their rafts across the Pacific.

Time Line

April 28, 1947
Thor Heyerdahl and his crew of five onboard *Kon-Tiki* leave Peru and are carried across the eastern Pacific by the prevailing winds

May–July 1947
During the expedition, the crew survive as the early navigators would have done

August 7, 1947
Kon-Tiki hits a reef at Raroia in the Tuamotu Islands

1970
Heyerdahl sails *Ra II* across the Atlantic

1978
Sails the *Tigris* from Iraq to Pakistan

What Next?

In 1969, Heyerdahl sailed Ra II, a reed boat across the Atlantic. In 1978, he sailed another reed boat, the Tigris, from Iraq to Pakistan, and then to Djibouti.

INTO AFRICA

By the early 1500s, the Portuguese had explored most of the African coastline, but the interior of the continent remained unknown to Europeans. They knew nothing of its great empires and kingdoms, and even less about its great rivers—the Nile, Niger, Congo, and Zambezi. In the late 18th century, European explorers set out to explore this great, unknown continent.

The course of the Niger

In 1788, Joseph Banks, who had sailed with Captain Cook on his first voyage to the Pacific, founded the Africa Association in London. One of the association's first acts was to commission Mungo Park to explore the Niger—the great river that ran through west Africa.

First sight of the river

Park arrived at the mouth of the Gambia River in 1795 and headed inland. He caught a fever, delaying the expedition for two months. He was then forced to travel with only two guides, because most local people refused to accompany him. Park was easy prey for the Muslim soldiers who captured him near the Senegal River and held him captive for five months. He escaped and made his way to Ségou on the banks of the Niger.

Mungo Park

Scot Mungo Park (1771–1806) was a medical officer for the East India Company. Joseph Banks asked Park to explore the Niger because he was impressed by his fine descriptions of new species of fish.

It's Amazing!

When he fell gravely ill, Park was nursed back to health by the inhabitants of a small village on the banks of the Niger.

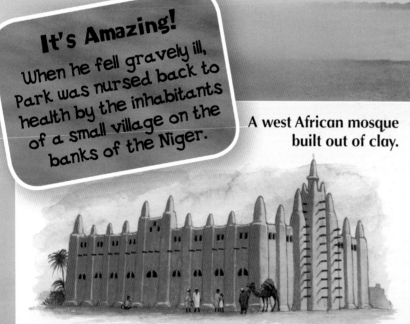

A west African mosque built out of clay.

Muslim lands

The Niger River flowed through the heartland of Muslim west Africa. The great Muslim Mali Empire had ruled the area from the 13th to the 17th centuries, and Timbuktu to the north of the river had been a major Islamic cultural center. Christians, such as Park, were unwelcome visitors.

Niger River

The Niger rises in the highlands of Guinea and flows northeast to Timbuktu in Mali before turning to empty into the Gulf of Guinea. Early European explorers were puzzled by the way it flowed away from the coast.

A canoe makes its way across the vast Niger River.

Death at the Falls

Back home, Park's account of his journey, *Travels in the Interior Districts of Africa*, brought him great fame. In 1805, he returned to follow the Niger along its entire length. He followed the river past Timbuktu, where it bends south. He paddled down to the Bussa Falls in present-day northern Nigeria. Here he was attacked by hostile locals, fell into the rapids, and drowned.

Time Line

July 1795
Park heads inland from mouth of the Gambia

February 1796
Park is captured by Arab soldiers

June 1796
Escapes and reaches Ségou on the Niger

April 1805
Park sets off on second expedition

August 1805
Sails down the Niger past Timbuktu

1806
At the Bussa Falls, Park is attacked and drowns in the river

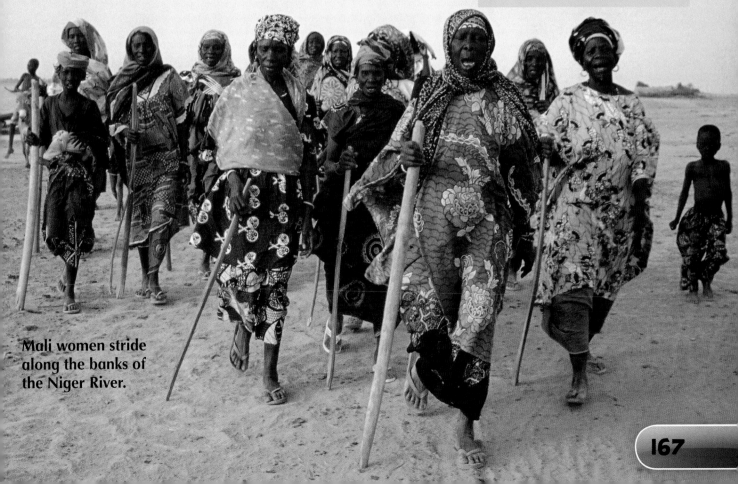

Mali women stride along the banks of the Niger River.

The Niger's end

Despite Park's two expeditions, the exact course of the Niger remained unknown, so a new expedition was organized. In 1822, British explorers Dixon Denham, Hugh Clapperton, and Walter Oudney set out from Tripoli, North Africa, to see if the river passed through the powerful sultanate (Muslim kingdom) of Kanem–Bornu around Lake Chad.

Hugh Clapperton

At 17, Scottish-born Clapperton (1788–1827) left home to join the navy. He had become a lieutenant by the time he was asked to join the expedition to the Niger. He was much praised for his opposition to slave trading in the region.

Sahara Desert

Tripoli

Muzuq

- – – – Oudney/Clapperton journey 1822–25
- – – – Clapperton/Lander journey 1825–27
- – – – Lander brothers' journey 1830
- ✝ Place of death

Timbuktu

Niger River

Katsina

Sokoto

Kano

Lake Chad

Yauri

✝ Clapperton 1827

✝ Oudney 1824

Kukawa

Bussa

Benue River

Badagri

Brass

✝ Lander 1834

Atlantic Ocean

Gulf of Guinea

Fernando Po

NW

W

Across the Sahara

After several arguments, Denham separated from Clapperton and Oudney, and these two become the first Europeans to see Lake Chad. The pair then set out to trace the Niger's path, but Oudney became ill and died. Clapperton met up with Denham and they returned to England.

Time Line

February 1822
Clapperton, Oudney, and Denham set off from Tripoli

February 1823
Clapperton and Oudney see Lake Chad

December 1825
Clapperton and Lander cross the Niger at Bussa

April 1827
Clapperton dies of dysentery

January 1830
Lander brothers set off for the Niger

November 1830
Landers are captured by Igbo and sold to a slave trader; Richard finishes his voyage paddling a royal canoe

The Igbo

As the Landers paddled down the Niger (see below), they were captured and held for ransom by the Igbo king. A slave trader bought the brothers and held John in captivity for a time. Richard worked as a slave on the 40-paddle royal canoe. It was on this canoe that Richard Lander completed the journey to the mouth of the Niger.

An elaborate ceremonial Igbo mask.

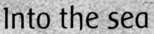

Into the sea

Accompanied by his servant, Richard Lemon Lander (1804–34), Clapperton returned to the Niger in 1825. He headed north from the Gulf of Guinea and traveled in a roundabout route to Sokoto. Here Clapperton died, and Lander headed back to London. Lander returned in 1830 with his brother John (1807–39).
Heading inland from Badagri, they reached the Niger upstream from Bussa and then paddled down the river. Richard made it to the estuary, proving that the Niger flowed into the Gulf of Guinea.

What Next?
Richard Lander returned to the Niger in 1832. His expedition was attacked and Lander was injured. He retreated to the island of Fernando Po, where he died.

Crossing the Sahara

Although Mungo Park had paddled past Timbuktu, it is unlikely he stopped at the city. It was closed to foreigners and its Muslim inhabitants would most probably have killed him and his crew. One Frenchman, however, was determined to visit this legendary "Queen of the Desert."

Traveling in disguise

René Caillié had twice visited west Africa and twice ended his journeys because of serious illness. The third time, in 1827, he was more successful. He disguised himself as an Egyptian Arab, which was easy because he was a fluent Arabic speaker. He then set off inland from Guinea with a small caravan of Mandingo traders heading for the Niger. Caillié said he was on his way home to Egypt and was treated well wherever he went.

René Caillié

As a child, René-Auguste Caillié (1799–1838) was obsessed with Africa. At 16, he became a cabin boy on a ship bound for the continent. He was later described as "one of the most reliable explorers of Africa."

A caravan of camels treks across the Sahara, carrying salt for sale.

Desert trade

For centuries, vast caravans of traders have crossed the Sahara. They take precious goods, such as gold and ostrich feathers, from cities, such as Timbuktu, to north Africa. They return south with salt, cloth, glass, ceramics, and horses.

Timbuktu

The city of Timbuktu lies a few hours' walk from the Niger. The city had once been a center for the teaching of Islam. It was entirely dependent on the Niger trade and the cross-Sahara caravans, which were controlled by nomadic Tuareg traders.

A traditional clay building in Timbuktu.

Only expert guides can navigate through the vast sand dunes of the Sahara.

Time Line

April 1827
Caillié joins a trading caravan heading inland at Rio Nunez

June 11, 1827
Reaches Timé, where he gets scurvy

January 9, 1828
Leaves on a caravan heading for Djenné

March 23, 1828
Sultan of Djenné gives Caillié a letter for Timbuktu merchants

April 20, 1828
Enters Timbuktu

May 4, 1828
Leaves Timbuktu and crosses the Sahara with a 1,400-strong camel caravan

It's Amazing!

In 1826, Scottish explorer Alexander Gordon Laing became the first European to visit Timbuktu. He was murdered by his guide soon after he left.

The disappointing city

In Timé, south of the Niger, Caillié joined a caravan heading north to Djenné on the Niger. He then joined a cargo boat heading downstream to Timbuktu. He entered the forbidden city in April 1828, but was disappointed to find a collection of mud huts, not the fabulous city he had imagined. He left Timbuktu after two weeks, crossing the Sahara to Morocco and safety.

Into the desert

After Caillié had paved the way, Europeans began to flock to the previously unknown and unexplored Sahara. One of the most successful of this wave of explorers was a German called Heinrich Barth.

Heinrich Barth

Heinrich Barth (1821–65) found it hard to get along with other people. As a child, he was sent to North Africa by his father in an attempt to improve his social skills. This failed, but it did give the young Heinrich a taste for travel.

The urge to head south

In 1844, Barth arrived in Morocco and traveled east along the Mediterranean coast to Alexandria in Egypt. He learned a lot from this journey, but he longed to head south into the desert. He returned to North Africa in 1850, this time intending to cross the Sahara. In Tripoli, Libya, he joined the English Mixed Scientific and Commercial Expedition, sponsored by the British government.

Barth (on the back of the camel) enters Timbuktu disguised as a holy man delivering religious books.

It's Amazing!

Barth spent so long in the desert that many in Europe thought he was dead. A relief party failed to find him, so his obituary was printed in the newspapers.

Time Line

March 1850
Barth joins expedition in Tripoli

April 1850
Discovers Roman ruins at Murzuq oasis

June 1850
Discovers Stone Age rock paintings in the Ahaggar mountains

April 1851
Explores area around Lake Chad

September 1853
Arrives in Timbuktu, where he stays for some months before returning to Lake Chad

September 1855
Arrives back in Tripoli

A Tuareg man wearing a tagelmust, a long cloth wrapped around the head and face.

The Tuareg

The Tuareg nomads of the mid 1800s survived the harsh conditions of the Sahara by raiding neighboring tribes and demanding money from cross-Sahara caravans. At first, the Tuareg were hostile to Barth, but eventually they let him pass through the desert.

The learned explorer

Barth was a historian, linguist, and geographer, as well as an explorer. He made detailed records about the lands he traveled through. Barth discovered Stone Age paintings in the desert that showed it had once been fertile land. He recorded 40 native dialects around Lake Chad. He also visited Timbuktu, confirming Caillié's view of the city (see pages 170–171).

North meets south

In 1851, Barth stayed in the prosperous trading city of Kano in what is now northern Nigeria. It was the center of extensive trading networks south to the coast, and north across the Sahara. Barth laid the groundwork for future European trade in the area.

The Kurmi market in Kano, founded in the 15th century and still used today.

Searching for the source

Much as the source and route of the Niger River preoccupied explorers in West Africa, the source of the Nile River fascinated explorers in East Africa. Everyone knew about its route through Egypt to the Mediterranean Sea, but where did this great river start?

James Bruce

Scotsman James Bruce (1730–94) started traveling after his wife died. He visited Spain and Portugal. When his father died four years later, he inherited enough money to travel full time. He first visited Africa in 1763.

Into Abyssinia

James Bruce was one of the first explorers to search for the source of the Nile. In 1768, he set off with about 20 men from Cairo up the Nile to the first set of cataracts (waterfalls) on the river at Aswan. He then headed east across the desert to the Red Sea. There, he hired a ship to take him to Massawa, in what is now Eritrea. The party then headed inland to Gondar, capital of Abyssinia (now Ethiopia). Here, he was granted the protection of the ruling emperor and helped in the country's civil war.

A mural of a wall devil in an Ethiopian Orthodox monastery on Lake Tana.

Land of monks

Lake Tana in northwest Ethiopia is fed by more than 60 streams, one of which is regarded as the source of the Blue Nile River. James Bruce recorded that there were as many as 45 inhabited islands on the lake, many with Christian monasteries on them.

Time Line

1768
Bruce and 20 men set off from Cairo up the Nile to Aswan and then overland to the Red Sea

1769
Sails down the Red Sea, stopping at Jeddah in Arabia before landing at Massawa and heading inland to Abyssinia

February 1770
Arrives in Gondar and gains protection from the Abyssinian emperor and his officials

November 1770
Reaches Lake Tana

At Lake Tana

From Gondar, Bruce headed south to Lake Tana, the source of the Blue Nile. Bruce considered the Blue Nile to be the main tributary of the Nile, so he thought he had discovered the source of the Nile River itself. In fact, he was wrong, because the White Nile is the main tributary, but Bruce was elated: "...standing in that spot which had baffled the genius, industry, and inquiry of both ancients and moderns for the course of near three thousand years. Though a mere private Briton, I have triumphed here."

The Blue Nile Falls, where the Blue Nile empties out of Lake Tana.

What Next?

When Bruce returned home, many people thought he had made up his stories about his journey. He was only believed when others visited the region.

To Lake Victoria

The ancient Greeks believed that the Nile River began in high mountains. In 1848, a German missionary saw a snow-capped mountain near the equator. This was the volcanic mountain Kilimanjaro. It had nothing to do with the Nile, but sparked interest in the source of the river.

The wrong lake

In 1856, the Royal Geographical Society in London sent an expedition to solve the mystery once and for all. Richard Burton and John Speke trekked from Zanzibar inland to Kazeh (Tabora) in western Tanzania. From here, they headed west to Ujiji on the shores of Lake Tanganyika. Burton had been convinced this was the source of the Nile, but found that no river flowed north out of the lake.

Richard Burton

Richard Burton (1821–90) was a controversial figure in the 19th century. He published more than 50 books, including a frank translation of the often raunchy Arabic tales *The Arabian Nights*.

John Hanning Speke

John Hanning Speke (1827–64) left home at 17 to join the British Indian Army. He spent most of his leave exploring the Himalayas. Speke first met Burton during an expedition to Somalia in 1854. He came close to death when tribesmen attacked them, but recovered to join Burton on their second expedition in 1857.

Marabou storks feed on the shores of Lake Tanganyika.

Lake Tanganyika

When Burton and Speke discovered Lake Tanganyika in 1858, only Burton saw it because disease had left Speke temporarily blind. The second largest lake in Africa, after Victoria, water from it flows via the Lukaga and Congo rivers to the Atlantic.

Finding Lake Victoria

The pair returned to Kazeh and then split up, Speke heading north. In July 1858, he discovered Lake Victoria and, although he had little proof, he was convinced the lake was the true source of the Nile. Speke reported his findings to the Royal Geographical Society, who agreed to fund another expedition.

Time Line

June 17, 1857
Burton and Speke head west from Zanzibar

December 1857
They set out for Ujiji

February 13, 1858
Reach Lake Tanganyika

April 1858
Burton rests in Ujiji and Speke heads north

July 30, 1858
Speke reaches Lake Victoria

1859
Back in London, Speke presents his theory about the source of the Nile before Burton, who disputes it, has returned from Africa

Fishermen in Lake Victoria, or Ukerewe, a vital source of food for the large population that lives near it.

What Next?

The local people called the lake Ukerewe, but Speke named it Lake Victoria in honor of the British queen.

Mission accomplished

John Speke was sure he had found the source of the Nile in Lake Victoria in 1858. Some people back in London, however, wanted more proof so he returned to Africa to find it.

The true source of the Nile

Speke set off in 1860 accompanied by James Grant. They traveled round the western edge of Lake Victoria. Grant was forced to rest due to an infected leg, so he was not with Speke in July 1862 when he found a waterfall at the northern end of the lake. It led down to a river—this was the start of the Nile.

James Grant

James Grant (1827–92) met John Speke while serving in the British army in India. After Speke's death, Grant defended his friend's achievements until Henry Stanley proved Speke right in 1875 (see pages 186–187).

Grant and Speke negotiate a safe passage with the Queen Dowager of Uganda.

Hippos are among the many animals that live in and by the White Nile.

The White Nile

The most distant stream of the White Nile (the major tributary of the Nile) starts in the Nyungwe Forest in southern Rwanda. It flows out of Lake Victoria and then north until it meets the Blue Nile at Khartoum. The river gets its name from the particles of whitish clay suspended in its waters.

Time Line

April 1860
Speke and Grant depart for East Africa

1861
Reach Kaweh and head north around western edge of Lake Victoria; Grant becomes ill

July 28, 1862
Speke discovers and names the Ripon Falls

February 1863
The two arrive in Gondokoro in Sudan, and meet Samuel and Florence Baker

March 1864
The Bakers discover the Murchison Falls and Lake Albert

September 15, 1864
Speke accidentally shoots himself

A tragic accident

Back in London, Speke and Grant were treated as heroes. But not everyone was convinced they had found the source of the Nile. Their most prominent critic was Richard Burton, who insisted that they had not proved that the river emerged from Lake Victoria. The pair agreed to debate the issue in public. The day before the debate, however, Speke accidentally shot himself.

Filling in the gaps

The Royal Geographical Society asked Samuel and Florence Baker to search for Speke and Grant, who had not been heard of for a year. After finding them, the Bakers explored parts of the Nile that Speke had not visited. They found that the river flows from Lake Victoria, down through the Murchison Falls, before heading north into Sudan.

The Murchison Falls, where the water is channeled through a 23-foot (7-m)-wide gap in the rocks.

Livingstone in Africa

David Livingstone was first and foremost a doctor and missionary, but he was also a superb explorer. The books he wrote about his four great journeys brought Africa to European attention. His fight against the Arab-run slave trade eventually ended that cruel practice.

It's Amazing!
In 1844, Livingstone was almost killed by a lion that "shook me as a terrier does a rat." He was left with many broken bones and 11 tooth marks in his left arm.

Time Line

March 14, 1841
Livingstone lands in Cape Town

1841–44
Explores Kalahari Desert

June 1849
Discovers Lake Ngami

April 1851
Discovers Zambezi

November 1853
Sets off west from the Zambezi

May 31, 1854
Reaches Luanda in Angola, then heads east

May 20, 1856
Reaches Quelimane on Indian Ocean

August 1859
Discovers Lake Nyasa on third expedition

First journey

Livingstone arrived in Cape Town in 1841. He headed inland to work at a Christian mission at Kuruman at the edge of the Kalahari Desert. Three years later, he moved farther north to set up his own mission. He took every opportunity to explore the area. He became the first European to see Lake Ngami in northern Botswana and, in 1851, the Zambezi—a previously unknown river. At this point, he accompanied his wife and four children back to Cape Town to send them back to England.

David Livingstone

Dr. David Livingstone (1813–73) was born into a poor family in Blantyre, Scotland. At the age of just 10 he was working 14 hours a day in a local cotton mill. He later worked part time in the mill while studying in Glasgow to be a doctor, so that he could become a medical missionary.

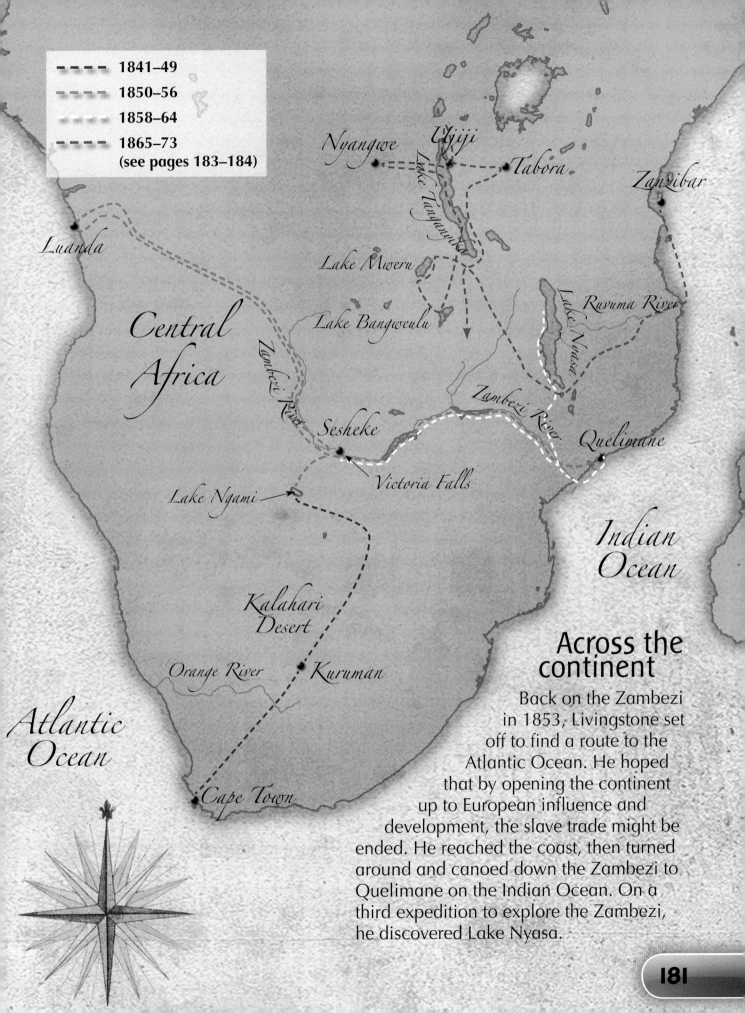

Indian Ocean

1841–49
1850–56
1858–64
1865–73
(see pages 183–184)

Nyangwe

Ujiji

Tabora

Zanzibar

Luanda

Lake Tanganyika

Lake Mweru

Ruvuma River

Lake Bangweulu

Lake Nyasa

Zambezi River

Sesheke

Zambezi River

Quelimane

Victoria Falls

Lake Ngami

Kalahari Desert

Orange River

Kuruman

Cape Town

Across the continent

Back on the Zambezi in 1853, Livingstone set off to find a route to the Atlantic Ocean. He hoped that by opening the continent up to European influence and development, the slave trade might be ended. He reached the coast, then turned around and canoed down the Zambezi to Quelimane on the Indian Ocean. On a third expedition to explore the Zambezi, he discovered Lake Nyasa.

Dr. Livingstone, I presume?

In 1865, David Livingstone set out on his fourth and final journey. This time his aim was to find the source of three great African rivers: the Congo, Zambezi, and Nile. John Speke had discovered the Nile's source, but many still doubted him. Livingstone set off to find out for himself.

A futile search

Livingstone started his journey on the Ruvuma River—the boundary between Tanzania and Mozambique—before trekking north to Lake Tanganyika. He spent the next three years exploring this and other lakes in the region and trying to work out which one was the source of the Nile. In fact, none was, because most of them drained into the Congo.

Livingstone became so ill that he often had to be carried on a stretcher by his companions.

The final journey

By the end of his life, Livingstone was weak with fever and becoming increasingly confused. For the first time ever, he got lost when his chronometers were accidentally damaged, and his sextant developed a fault. But he was still driven to travel in his quest to end the slave trade.

A 19th-century painting based on Livingstone description of the moment he and Stanley first met.

Lechwe, a kind of antelope, near Lake Bangweulu, where Livingstone died.

Livingstone's end

When Livingstone died, his companions Chuma and Susi carried his body 600 miles (1,000 km) to the coast so that it could be taken to Great Britain. As he had requested, his heart was buried under a tree in a village near Lake Bangweulu.

A famous meeting

Livingstone had been out of touch with the rest of the world since 1869, so in 1871 an American newspaper hired Henry Stanley to seek him out. The pair met on November 10, 1871, at Ujiji. Stanley later reported that he was so overwhelmed, he took off his hat and uttered the famous words: "Dr. Livingstone, I presume?"

Time Line

March 22, 1866
Livingstone lands on East African coast

August 8, 1866
Reaches Lake Nyasa

April 1, 1867
Livingstone reaches Lake Tanganyika

November 1867
Reaches Lake Mweru

July 18, 1868
First sees Lake Bangweulu

March 29, 1871
Arrives in Nyangwe, the most northerly point in his travels

November 10, 1871
Meets Stanley at Ujiji

May 1, 1873
Livingstone dies near Lake Bangweulu

What Next?

A month after Livingstone's death, the British closed down the slave market in Zanzibar, the busiest in Africa.

Livingstone's legacy

Although Livingstone did not discover the source of any major river, end the slave trade, or establish permanent missions, he did add a vast amount to European knowledge of Africa. He discovered several lakes and charted the Zambezi and other rivers. Soon after his death, the slave trade dramatically declined.

A statue of Livingstone at Victoria Falls.

183

Meeting Stanley

By 1871, Dr. Livingstone had been in Africa for 30 years and had traveled many thousands of miles. He was old, ill, and unable to cope with the lengthy marches from place to place. His servants often had to carry him on a stretcher, but he was determined to continue. In this extract from his diary, Livingstone describes his feelings on first meeting Stanley.

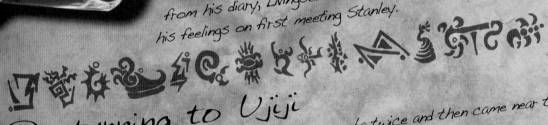

Returning to Ujiji

SEPTEMBER 23 We now crossed the River Longumba twice and then came near the great mountain mass on the west of Lake Tanganyika. From here to Tanganyika is about ten days' march through open forest. I was sorely ill by this march back to Ujiji. By the end of it I felt as if dying on my feet. Almost every step in pain, my appetite failed, while my mind, sorely depressed, acted on my body.

OCTOBER 8 The road covered with fragments of quartz was very sore to my feet, which were crammed into ill-made French shoes. How the bare feet of the men and women stood out, I don't know.

The "good Samaritan"

NOVEMBER When my spirits were at their lowest ebb, the good Samaritan was close at hand, for one morning Susi came running at the top of his speed and gasped out, "An Englishman, I see him!" and off he darted to meet him.

The American flag at the head of the caravan told me of the nationality of the stranger. Baths of tin, huge kettles, cooking pots, and tents made me think "This must be a luxurious traveler, and not one at his wits' end like me." It was Henry Moreland Morton Stanley, the traveling correspondent to the New York Herald He had been sent by James Gordon Bennett, at an expense of more than 4,000 pounds, to find out accurate information about me, and if dead to bring home my bones. The news he had to tell to one who had been two full years without any tidings from Europe made my whole frame thrill.

Appetite returned, and instead of the spare, tasteless, two meals a day I ate four times daily, and in a week began to feel strong. But this kindness of Mr. Bennett, so nobly carried into effect by Mr. Stanley, was simply overwhelming. I really do feel extremely grateful, and at the same time I am a little ashamed at not being more worthy of the generosity.

The exploration of the Congo

Henry Stanley was a very different man from Livingstone. He was an adventurer, not an explorer, interested solely in fame and fortune. Livingstone often traveled almost alone, but Stanley commanded large, armed groups.

Across Africa

Stanley set off in 1874 to explore the Congo River. He left from Zanzibar and headed to Lake Victoria, which he sailed around in a collapsible canoe, the *Lady Alice*. He sailed down the Congo, often coming under attack from hostile locals and setting fire to their villages in revenge. In 1877, he reached the Atlantic coastline and sent stories of his trip to European newspapers.

Stanley's boat, the *Lady Alice*, was collapsible so that it could be carried around rapids.

Henry Stanley

Henry Morton Stanley (1841–1904) was born John Rowlands in North Wales. He moved to New Orleans in his teens, and eventually took a job as a reporter for the *New York Herald*, who sent him to find Livingstone.

Settling the Congo

Stanley colonized the Congo on behalf of Leopold II of Belgium. He negotiated treaties with local chiefs and explored the lands either side of the river. He earned the nickname "Bula Matari" ("Rock Breaker") for his harsh treatment of those who worked for him.

A chief of the Molunga, a tribe who signed a treaty with Stanley, which they were later to regret under Leopold II's harsh rule.

Time Line

March 14, 1872
Stanley leaves Livingstone

1874
Sets out from Zanzibar

January 1875
Reaches Lake Victoria

October 1876
Reaches Lualaba River and heads down river

August 1877
Reaches Atlantic coast

1879–84
Colonizes the Congo

1888
Finds Emin Pasha at Lake Albert

What Next?

Leopold II ran the Congo Free State. The Belgian government forced him to hand it over in 1908 due to his terrible treatment of its people. The country gained its independence in 1960.

Stanley the colonialist

King Leopold II paid Stanley to colonize the Congo because he was desperate to have an African colony. Stanley did this in five years from 1879, creating the Congo Free State. On his final mission, Stanley rescued Emin Pasha, the governor of southern Sudan, who was under siege from rebel forces.

A goliath tigerfish, one of the many dangerous fish that live in the Congo River.

The Congo River

The vast Congo River starts as the Lualaba River in the mountains of southern Congo, and flows for about 2,900 miles (4,700 km) in a loop until it reaches the Atlantic Ocean. Rapids near its mouth make it difficult to reach from the sea.

A woman alone

Almost without exception, the explorers of Africa were men. Mary Kingsley, however, broke all the rules of her time and became one of the most important explorers of West Africa.

The late starter

Kingsley was the daughter of a widely traveled doctor, but she herself had rarely left home before her first expedition to Africa. She had no formal education, so she asked the British Museum which natural history subjects she should study. They suggested she collect specimens of beetles and fish. She quickly learned navigation and other skills, and fell in love with the people of Africa.

Time Line

August 1893
Kingsley sets sail from England onboard the cargo ship *Lagos*, reaching as far south as Angola

January 1894
Returns to Great Britain, and the British Museum agree to fund her next expedition

November 1894
Explores the Ogowe River in Gabon before trekking to the Rembwe River

September 1895
Climbs Mount Cameroon

November 1895
Returns to London and writes about her travels

Kingsley traveled in full Victorian dress and carried an umbrella, which she used to scare off nosy hippos!

Mary Kingsley

Mary Kingsley (1862–1900) spent most of her life at home caring for her invalid mother. Only when her parents both died was she able to fulfill her desire to travel. After her two explorations, she returned to Africa to nurse British soldiers in the Boer War and died of fever.

Earning respect

Kingsley's first expedition down the west coast of Africa proved her worth as an explorer, and the British Museum agreed to support another expedition in 1894. She became the first person to travel through much of Gabon and the first woman to climb Mount Cameroon. Kingsley often traveled alone, trading with local tribes. She always made sure she never drank unboiled water, which kept her free from many diseases.

The foothills of Mount Cameroon, which Mary Kingsley climbed in 1895.

Kingsley studied the belief systems of African shamans, or holy men.

It's a Mystery!

When she climbed Mount Cameroon, Kingsley's guides deserted her midway, so she made the final ascent by herself.

Enlightened traveler

Mary Kingsley did not share the racist views of many of her fellow European explorers. She was, therefore, better able to understand the African cultures she studied. She insisted that Africans were every bit as cultured and advanced as Europeans.

Wildlife adventures

Kingsley was often fearless of the risks she faced, both from the people that she encountered and from the continent's dangerous animals. She hit an attacking leopard over the head with a water pot and rescued another from a trap. She also had close encounters with crocodiles.

Kingsley was not afraid of Africa's dangerous wildlife, including leopards.

EXTREME EXPLORATION

By the start of the 20th century, most of the world's land had been explored and mapped. However, the polar regions remained unconquered. Explorers also found new challenges by diving in the oceans and descending to their greatest depths, and climbing the highest mountains. With the arrival of space travel, we have been able to explore our moon and, using unmanned craft, our solar system and the stars beyond it.

The race to the North Pole

By the middle of the 19th century, the coastline of the Arctic Ocean was known to explorers. But they had yet to reach the very top of the world—the North Pole. The race to get there first soon began in earnest.

Fridtjof Nansen

Norwegian Nansen (1861–1930) was a skilled Arctic explorer who planned his missions with great care. He became a diplomat in later life and was awarded the Nobel Prize for Peace in 1922.

Ever farther north

One of the first Polar explorers was the American Charles Hall (1821–71) who, during three expeditions, sailed farther north than anyone before. He was the first person to visit the north shore of Greenland. Hall used the techniques of the local Inuit to help him survive, but he became ill and died onboard his ship *Polaris*.

The *Fram* was built to withstand the pressure of the ice.

The reinforced ship

In 1884, objects from a ship that had sunk off Siberia were found on the other side of the Arctic Ocean in Greenland. They were carried there by currents in the Arctic Ocean. This find gave Nansen the idea of floating to the North Pole. His ship, the *Fram*, was specially built using thick wood reinforced with metal.

A tragic flight

Swedish engineer Salomon Andrée (1854–97) tried to fly to the North Pole in a hot-air balloon. In July 1897, he took off from Spitsbergen in his balloon *Ornen* (*Eagle*), but it disappeared after two days. The wreckage of the balloon and the bodies of Andrée and his two companions were found on the ice.

Andrée and his copilots stand in front of their balloon on Spitsbergen.

Floating in the ice

In 1893, Fridtjof Nansen set out on his remarkable expedition. He sailed his ship, the *Fram,* into the pack ice and hoped that the Arctic currents would take his ice-bound ship to the North Pole. The ship remained frozen in for two years before Nansen realized it would miss the Pole. He and a companion then tried unsuccessfully to walk the rest of the way.

Ice forms a solid mass across much of the Arctic Ocean.

It's Amazing!

While on the Fram, Nansen found that the Arctic Ocean was both much deeper and warmer than expected. He proved there was no land mass under the North Pole.

Time Line

August 1871
Hall sails up the west coast of Greenland and rides a sled 200 miles (320 km) on pack ice toward the North Pole

June 26, 1893
Nansen sets sail on the *Fram*

September 20, 1893
The *Fram* is frozen in and pushed northeast by the ocean current

March 14, 1895
Nansen and Frederick Johansen set off with dogsleds, reaching farther north than anyone else before, but are forced to turn back

July 1897
Andrée attempts to fly to the North Pole in a hot-air balloon

Reaching the Pole

The race for the North Pole carried on into the early years of the 20th century. It was eventually won by the American explorer Robert Peary in 1909. Controversy continues to rage around his achievement, however, with some historians doubting he ever reached the Pole at all.

Preparing for the Pole

In a series of expeditions starting in 1886, Robert Peary pushed farther north. Each time he learned more about how to survive in the Arctic. By 1909, he was ready for the final attempt. The clothes, sleeping quarters, food, dogs, and sleds had all been chosen specially for this expedition. The 24-man team left base camp on Ellesmere Island in March 1909, and set up a series of supply camps along two-thirds of the route to the Pole.

Robert Peary

Robert Peary (1836–1920) devoted himself to Arctic exploration for a quarter of a century. He had trained as a civil engineer and worked for the navy before beginning his Arctic quest. He paid for his expeditions by writing about his adventures in books and magazines.

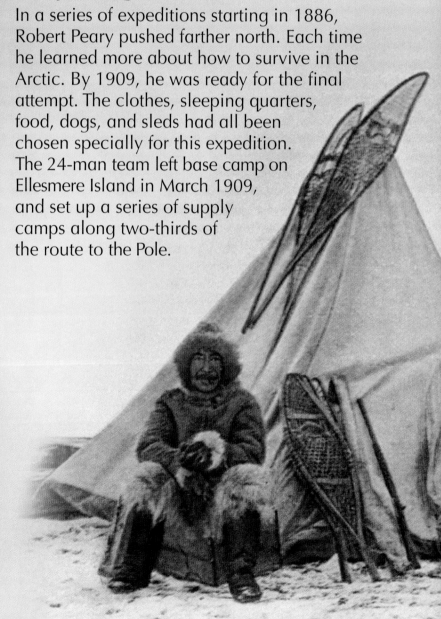

Matthew Henson

Matthew Henson (1866–1955) was an African American born into poverty. At first, Henson worked for Peary as a valet but he soon took responsibility for organizing his expeditions.

Racing there and back

The expedition traveled quickly over the hard ice, allowing Peary, Henson, and four local Inuit to make the final 155 miles (250 km) to the Pole. After five days, on April 6, 1909, they set up camp 3 miles (5 km) from the Pole. They crossed the Pole the next day before heading back to Cape Columbia, covering 70 miles (112 km) in one day. Some doubt that Peary could travel at such a speed.

This drawing was made from a photograph taken by Peary of the four Inuit in the team that reached the Pole.

Time Line

April 1908
Peary and his expedition drop anchor near Cape Sheridan on Ellesmere Island; they then build a base camp farther north at Cape Columbia

March 1, 1909
The expedition leaves base camp

April 2
Peary, Henson, and four Inuit make the final dash to the Pole

April 6
Establish camp just short of the Pole

April 7
Peary stays in the area for 30 hours to make the calculations to prove he is at the Pole

April 23
Peary and team return to base camp

What Next?
If Peary did not really reach the Pole, the first man who did was the British explorer Wally Herbert in 1969.

The first exploration of Antarctica

Captain Cook sailed into Antarctic waters in 1773 but this vast, cold, inhospitable continent remained virtually unseen for another 70 years. Its landmass was hard to find, because it was overlapped with a huge ice sheet that spread out into the sea.

Carstens Borchgrevink

Norwegian Carstens Borchgrevink (1864–1934) was the first person to land on Antarctica. As part of a group searching for new whaling waters, he landed near Cape Adare in Victoria Land on January 24, 1895.

Breaking through the ice

Sir James Ross (1800–62) was an extremely experienced English polar explorer. In 1841, he managed to steer his two ships, the *Terror* and *Erebus*, through the pack ice that surrounds the continent. He then sailed into the sea that is now named after him, but he was unable to land on the continent itself.

Ross and his crew land on Possession Island.

Ice and fire

On January 12, 1841, James Ross came close to Antarctica when he landed on an icy island off Victoria Land. He named it Possession Island. Two weeks later he sighted an active volcano, which he named Mt. Erebus.

An Antarctic winter

In February 1899, Carstens Borchgrevink arrived off Cape Adare onboard the *Southern Cross*, a Norwegian whaling ship. He landed with a small scientific team, including a meteorologist and a naturalist. His team also included two Lapps from northern Norway, who were experts at surviving in cold conditions. The team built a hut and survived a whole winter in the continent.

A drawing made by team cook Kolbein Ellefsen in the hut where they spent the winter.

Ross's ships HMS *Terror* and HMS *Erebus* sail past Mt. Erebus.

Time Line

1820
Two separate ships sight Antarctica

January 9, 1841
Ross's two ships breach the pack ice and he discovers Victoria Land

January 28, 1841
Ross sights an active volcano on Ross Island

January 24, 1895
Borchgrevink sets foot on Antarctica

1899
Borchgrevink and a scientific team spend winter in Antarctica

Race to the Pole

With the North Pole reached in 1909, only the South Pole remained unconquered. Its harsh, unforgiving climate had already defeated several expeditions, but in 1910 two well-equipped teams set out for the pole. It was to be a race to the death.

The race begins

The first team was led by Roald Amundsen, the Norwegian hero of the Northwest Passage (see pages 78–79). Leaving the Bay of Whales on the east side of the Ross Sea on October 19, 1911, he headed across the ice shelf and up to the polar plateau. Just under two weeks later, a British expedition led by Robert Scott set out from the western end of the Ross Sea in McMurdo Sound and made their way onto the plateau.

Robert Scott

Captain Scott (1868–1912) was already an experienced Antarctic explorer by the time he set off for the Pole in 1911. He had taken part in a major expedition with Ernest Shackleton in 1901–4.

A heavy load

Robert Scott's expedition was not as well prepared as Amundsen's and relied mainly on Siberian ponies to pull their supplies. The ponies soon died of cold, forcing his team to pull the supplies on skis. Amundsen used skills learned from the Inuit in the Arctic and took huskies instead.

Scott's party pull their heavy sleds across the ice.

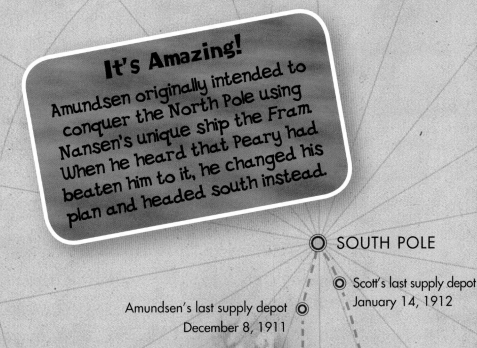

It's Amazing!

Amundsen originally intended to conquer the North Pole using Nansen's unique ship the Fram. When he heard that Peary had beaten him to it, he changed his plan and headed south instead.

Time Line

October 19, 1911
Amundsen's team sets off from Bay of Whales

November 1, 1911
Scott's team leave their base by McMurdo Sound

December 14, 1911
Amundsen and team reach the South Pole

January 11, 1912
Amundsen returns to base camp

January 17, 1912
Scott reaches the Pole

March 17, 1912
The sick Captain Oates walks out of the camp to die in the snow

March 29, 1912
Scott and two remaining companions die

SOUTH POLE

Scott's last supply depot
January 14, 1912

Amundsen's last supply depot
December 8, 1911

Polar Plateau

Transantarctic Mountains

ANTARCTICA

Ross Ice Shelf

Scott's last camp
March 19, 1912

Bay of Whales

McMurdo Sound

ROSS SEA

A Norwegian triumph

Amundsen's better preparations gave him the edge over Scott. His team arrived first at the Pole on December 14, 1911. They were back at their base camp by the time Scott reached the Pole on January 17, 1912. Tired and despondent, Scott and his team all died on the return journey, the last three within only 11 miles (18 km) of safety.

 Amundsen's team

Scott's team

Crossing Antarctica

Ernest Shackleton tried to reach the South Pole in 1908. He got as far as the magnetic South Pole (where Earth's magnetic field points directly upward—96 miles (155 km) from the geographic Pole), then turned back. In 1915, he returned with an even more ambitious plan.

Ernest Shackleton

Shackleton (1874–1922) first went to the Antarctic in 1901. After his two expeditions of 1908 and 1915, he returned in 1921 to explore Enderby Land, but died in South Georgia before he could reach it.

The *Endurance* finally sinks into the ice in October 1915.

Coast to coast

Shackleton's plan was to cross the continent from the Weddell Sea to the Ross Sea. But it almost failed before it started, because World War I broke out in Europe just as he was about to set sail from England. Shackleton offered his two ships, *Endurance* and *Aurora*, for war duty, but was instructed to continue with his expedition.

Mawson's disaster

In 1911, Douglas Mawson led an Australian expedition to explore the Antarctic coastline. One of his team plunged into a crack in the ice with almost all the food. Mawson reached base camp only to find the supply ship had just left. He was only rescued at the end of the winter.

Mawson and companion Xavier Mertz struggle through the snow.

Trapped

The *Endurance* arrived in the Weddell Sea in January 1915, and was immediately trapped in pack ice. After 10 months, it sank. Shackleton and his party sailed to Elephant Island in the lifeboats. From there, he and five others set sail to seek help. They reached South Georgia and returned to rescue the rest of his team.

It's Amazing!
Shackleton never lost a single man in the Antarctic, a rare achievement in Polar exploration.

One of the snow tractors used by Fuchs to cross Antarctica.

Success!

Antarctica was finally crossed from coast to coast in 1958 when an expedition led by Vivian Fuchs crossed from the Weddell to the Ross seas. He used snow tractors, and he had the benefit of icebreakers, radios, heaters, and a base at the South Pole itself—none of which were available to Shackleton.

Time Line

December 1913
Mawson is rescued after surviving two Antarctic winters

January 1915
Endurance enters the Weddell Sea, where it is trapped in pack ice

October 27, 1915
Endurance sinks and the crew sail to Elephant Island

August 30, 1916
Shackleton returns to rescue the expedition on Elephant Island

March 2, 1958
Fuchs completes first successful crossing of Antarctica

Shackleton's Antarctic diary

In 1908, Ernest Shackleton and three others set off for the South Pole, but stopped 96 miles (155 km) short. They were the first humans to reach the Polar plateau. These are extracts from his diary.

DECEMBER 30
We only did 4 miles 100 yards today. We started at 7 a.m. but had to camp at 11 a.m., a blizzard springing up from the south. It is very annoying.

DECEMBER 31
The hardest day we have had, pushing through soft snow uphill with a strong head wind and drift all day. We are all feeling bad for lack of food.

JANUARY 4
The end is in sight. We can only go for three more days at the most, for we are weakening rapidly. Short food and a blizzard wind from the south, with driving drift, have plainly told us today that we are reaching our limit.

JANUARY 6
This must be our last outward march with the sled and camp equipment. Tomorrow we must leave camp with some food, and push as far south as possible.

JANUARY 9
Our last day outward. We looked south, but could see nothing but the dead white snow plain.

The voyage of the *Challenger*

Oceans cover seven tenths of the Earth, but before the mid 1800s surprisingly little was known about what lay beneath the surface. In 1872, a remarkable expedition set sail to investigate on a ship that had been specially adapted for scientific research.

John Murray

Canadian John Murray (1844–1914) served as Charles Thomson's assistant on the *Challenger* expedition. He edited and published the 50 volumes of reports that appeared later.

Scientists at work in the biology laboratory on the *Challenger*.

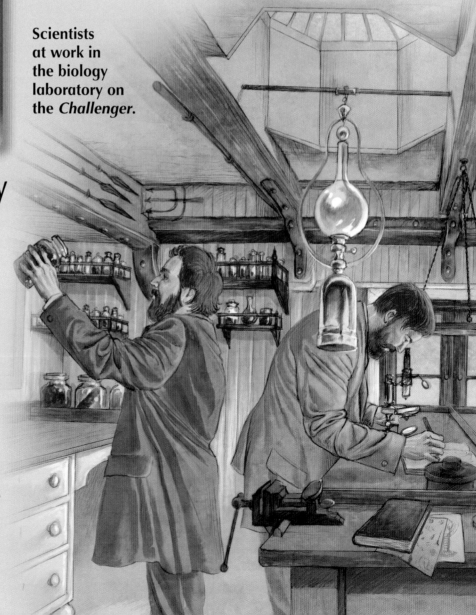

Floating laboratory

The idea for the expedition came from Charles Wyville Thomson (1830–92), professor of zoology at Edinburgh University. He persuaded the British Royal Navy to loan him HMS *Challenger*, a steam-powered warship. Her guns and some masts were removed to make more room for laboratories and cabins, and a dredging platform was added to take samples from the seabed.

The diving bell

In 1690, Edmund Halley invented a bell that let divers work under water. The wooden bell was covered with lead to make it sink and filled with air pumped down through leather pipes from the surface. Four people could stay at a depth of 59 feet (18 m) for 90 minutes.

A wealth of knowledge

The *Challenger* set sail in 1872 and remained at sea for four years, crossing every ocean except the Arctic. During the course of the expedition, it sailed 79,200 miles (127,500 km) and discovered 4,717 new species of marine life. When its reports were published, their editor, John Murray, described them as "the greatest advance in knowledge of our planet since the celebrated discoveries of the 15th century."

Time Line

1690
Edmund Halley invents the diving bell

1797
C. H. Kleingert invents early, rigid diving suit

1819
August Siebe invents a more flexible suit with a heavy metal helmet

1855
First textbook on oceanography (science of the oceans) published

December 21, 1872
HMS *Challenger* sets sail from Portsmouth

1876
Challenger expedition ends

Diving suits

One of the first diving suits was invented in 1797 by the German C. H. Kleingert, who enclosed the diver's upper body in a cylinder. Later suits let the diver swim around more easily. Air was pumped to the diver inside a heavy metal helmet. The pressure of the air escaping from the helmet prevented water from flooding into it.

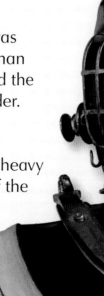

To the bottom of the oceans

It is difficult for divers to operate deep under the sea, because the pressure on a diver's lungs is intense and the water is cold and dark. As a result, the deep seas remained almost entirely unknown until a new invention made underwater exploration possible in the 1930s.

Time Line

June 6, 1930
The bathysphere makes its first deep-sea dive off Nonsuch Island in Bermuda

1934
Barton and Beebe make a world record descent of 3,028 feet (923 m) off Bermuda, a record for 15 years

1953
The bathyscaphe *Trieste* is launched in Italy

January 23, 1960
With Auguste Piccard's son Jacques and Don Walsh of the U.S. Navy onboard, the *Trieste* reaches the ocean floor of the Challenger Deep —the deepest part of the Mariana Trench

The bathysphere

The bathysphere was developed in 1930 by two Americans—the scientist William Beebe and the diver Otis Barton. It consisted of a metal sphere lowered into the water on a steel cable attached to a surface ship. Once they are sealed inside, the divers breathe oxygen from a high-pressure cylinder. They made their first descent in the waters off Bermuda in 1930.

William Beebe (left) and Otis Barton next to the bathysphere.

William Beebe

William Beebe (1877–1962) was curator of ornithology at the New York Zoological Society, but he was interested in far more than just birds. He made 35 dives in the bathysphere to observe the marine life of the Atlantic Ocean.

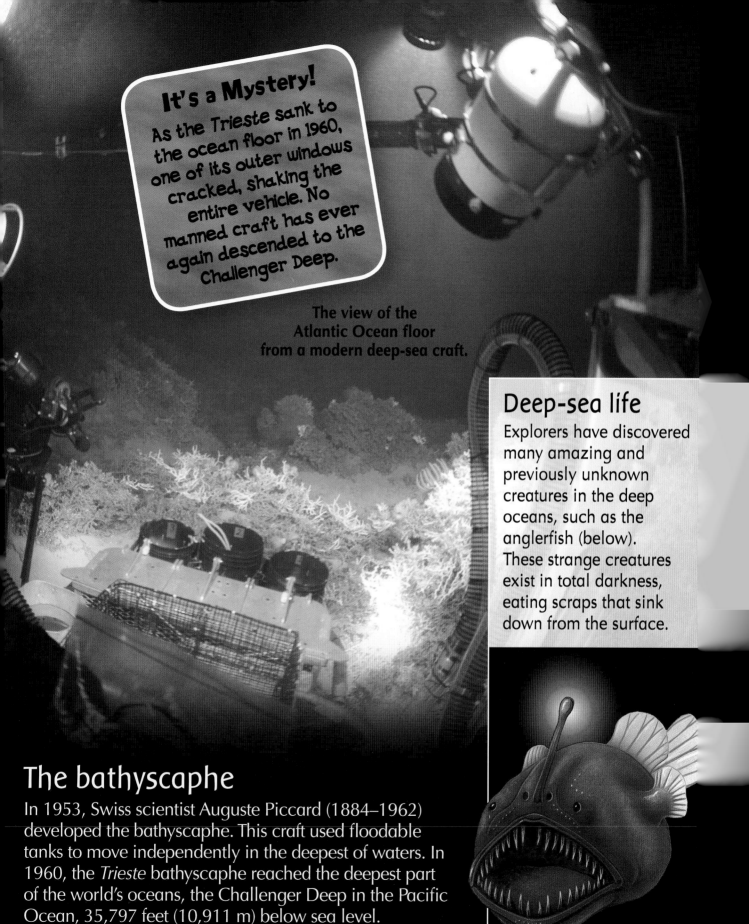

It's a Mystery!

As the Trieste sank to the ocean floor in 1960, one of its outer windows cracked, shaking the entire vehicle. No manned craft has ever again descended to the Challenger Deep.

The view of the Atlantic Ocean floor from a modern deep-sea craft.

Deep-sea life

Explorers have discovered many amazing and previously unknown creatures in the deep oceans, such as the anglerfish (below). These strange creatures exist in total darkness, eating scraps that sink down from the surface.

The bathyscaphe

In 1953, Swiss scientist Auguste Piccard (1884–1962) developed the bathyscaphe. This craft used floodable tanks to move independently in the deepest of waters. In 1960, the *Trieste* bathyscaphe reached the deepest part of the world's oceans, the Challenger Deep in the Pacific Ocean, 35,797 feet (10,911 m) below sea level.

The world beneath the waves

Just below the ocean waves is a beautiful world of fish, sea mammals, coral reefs, and marine plant life. Until very recently that world was closed to us. One man more than any other made it possible for people to explore beneath the waves.

A portable air supply

In 1943 the French underwater explorer Jacques Cousteau, working with the engineer Emile Gagnan, invented the aqualung, a portable air supply carried on a diver's back. The invention enabled Cousteau to explore the underwater world, taking photographs of the wonderful sights he saw.

It's Amazing!

Cousteau was fascinated by the idea of living underwater. In 1963, he built an underwater house in the Red Sea and lived in it for a month.

Thanks to Cousteau, divers are able to experience the beauty of coral reefs, such as this one in the Red Sea.

Jacques Cousteau

French naval officer Jacques-Yves Cousteau (1910–97) became fascinated by the water at an early age. After World War II, when he fought for the French Resistance, he set up his own underwater research company.

The *Calypso*'s condition is deteriorating as Cousteau's relatives argue over its fate.

A disputed legacy

Cousteau's boat the *Calypso* was built for the British Royal Navy. He turned it into a base for his diving. Since Cousteau's death, ownership of the *Calypso* has been disputed and it has not been used.

Revealing a new world

Cousteau's underwater photography of the coral reefs of the Red Sea was the first detailed investigation of sea life. His 1956 movie *The Silent World* was the first color underwater film to be shown to a wide audience. Throughout his life, Cousteau was interested in educating people about the underwater environment. In 1985, he began a long-term research project to examine the health of the world's oceans and seas.

A diver explores inside a shipwreck with the help of an aqualung.

The aqualung

The aqualung was the world's first self-contained diving unit. The high-pressure air supply is carried on the diver's back in cylinders, and reaches the diver via a tube connected to a mouthpiece. The aqualung allows divers to swim freely to a depth of 98 feet (30 m) without restrictive cables or a heavy diving suit.

Time Line

1938
Cousteau first dives in the Mediterranean

1943
Invents the aqualung with Emile Gagnan

1950
Acquires the *Calypso*

1952–53
Makes pioneering photographic study of the Red Sea

1963
Lives underwater for a month

1973
Founds Cousteau Society for the Protection of Ocean Life

1985
Starts research project into the state of the world's oceans

The top of the world

The high mountains of the Himalayas in Asia have long fascinated European explorers. Different nations concentrated on different Himalayan peaks: the Germans on Nanga Parbat, the Italians on K2—the second highest mountain in the world—and the British on Everest—the highest of them all.

Preparing the way

In the years after the end of World War I in 1918, 13 expeditions attempted—and failed—to reach the summit of Everest, all from the Tibetan side. In 1949, Nepal opened up its borders to Europeans, allowing climbers to tackle Everest from its side of the border. The following year, French climbers reached the top of Annapurna I, breaking the psychological 26,250 feet (8,000 m) barrier. The way was now clear to tackle Everest.

Time Line

March 10, 1953
Expedition led by John Hunt leaves Katmandu and treks through the Himalayan foothills

March 25
Expedition sets up base camp on the Khunbu glacier at 18,145 feet (5,530 m)

May 28
Hillary and Tenzing set off; support team stops at 28,051 feet (8,550 m)

May 29
Hillary and Tenzing reach the summit at 11:30 a.m. and spend 15 minutes there before descending

Tenzing and Hillary

Tenzing Norgay (1914– 86), left, was a Nepalese with a vast experience of Himalayan climbing. He reached to within 820 feet (250 m) of the summit with a Swiss expedition in 1952. Edmund Hillary (1919–2008), right, was born in Auckland, New Zealand, and climbed his first major mountain at the age of 20. In 1950, he climbed in the Alps and made his first visit to the Himalayas in 1951.

Reaching the summit

The expedition in 1953 was carefully planned, with a series of supply camps established up to the South Crest at 28,051 feet (8,550 m). From there, two climbers would climb the final 984 feet (300 m) to the summit. Accompanied by a support group, Edmund Hillary and Tenzing Norgay set out on May 28, spending that night on a narrow, snow-covered ledge. The next morning was clear as the pair climbed to the summit.

Mount Everest, at 29,035 feet (8,850 m), is the highest mountain in the world.

A supply camp on a modern expedition to climb Everest.

Supply camps

The 1953 expedition established a series of nine camps between base camp at the foot of the Khunbu glacier and the summit. Each camp was supplied with food and equipment necessary for the climb, including oxygen tanks for the climbers.

It's Amazing!

Since the conquest of Everest in 1953, the mountain has been climbed almost every year. On May 15, 2002, 54 climbers reached the summit on the same day.

Mountain guides

Tenzing Norgay was a Sherpa. The Sherpa are an ethnic group from the Himalayan region of Nepal. Their ancestors migrated to Nepal from eastern Tibet about 500 years ago. The Sherpa are tough, hardy people well used to the high altitudes of the Himalayas, and they are valuable guides and porters on mountaineering expeditions in the region.

The Sherpa are used to making long journeys on foot at high altitudes.

Into space

The attention of many potential explorers turned toward the heavens and into space after 1945. The technological advances required to send a man into orbit around the world, let alone to the Moon, and then bring him safely back to Earth were immense.

The Space Race

Near the end of the World War II, Germany had developed the technology to fire V-2 rockets at supersonic speeds within Earth's atmosphere. Once the war ended, scientists used this technology to build rockets capable of escaping Earth's gravity and traveling through space. A competition began between the United States and the USSR (now Russia) to put a man into space.

Time Line

October 4, 1957
USSR launches the world's first artificial satellite, *Sputnik I*

November 1957
A dog called Laika is the first living creature in space on *Sputnik II*, but dies in orbit

August 20, 1960
Sputnik V carries two dogs into orbit, and brings them back to Earth safely

April 12, 1961
Yuri Gagarin becomes the first person in space, orbiting the Earth once onboard *Vostok I*

Yuri Gagarin

Yuri Gagarin (1934–68) was born in western Russia and qualified as a military pilot in 1957. He was chosen along with 19 other cosmonauts in 1960 to join the Soviet space program. His successful space flight in 1961 made him into an international celebrity. He died on a military training flight seven years later.

Two firsts

The USSR launched the world's first artificial satellite (object that orbits Earth), *Sputnik I*, in 1957. Four years later, cosmonaut Yuri Gagarin was the first man to be sent into space on board a *Vostok* spaceship. The United States sent its first astronaut, Alan Shepard, into space a few months after Gagarin, but the USSR had established a clear lead in the Space Race.

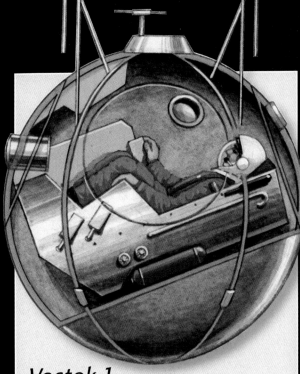

Earth seen from space.

It's Amazing!

The first two living creatures to survive going into space and reentering Earth's atmosphere were the dogs Belka and Strelka in 1960.

Vostok 1

The spherical *Vostok* spacecraft that took Yuri Gagarin into space was launched from the Baikonur Cosmodrome. The flight lasted 108 minutes. It ended when Gagarin ejected from the capsule. He was 4 miles (7 km) above the ground and had to parachute to safety.

Sputnik 1

Sputnik I was launched on top of a rocket from the Baikonur Cosmodrome in what is now Kazakhstan on October 4, 1957. The spherical satellite only measured 23 inches (58.5 cm) in diameter. It traveled at 18,000 mph (29,000 km/h) and broadcast radio signals for 22 days until its transmitter batteries ran out.

A man on the Moon

In May 1961, President John Kennedy committed the United States to landing a man on the Moon by the end of the decade. The Americans were behind the Soviet Union in the space race, so the Apollo space program was devised to help them catch up.

The Apollo program

The Apollo space program was the most ambitious project any nation had undertaken in peacetime. At its peak, almost half a million people worked for it. Their goal was to design a craft that would carry three human beings to the Moon, 236,100 miles (380,000 km) away.

Apollo 11 was launched on the 365-foot (111-m)-tall, three-stage Saturn V rocket.

Tragic beginnings

The first launch in 1967 was a disaster. The three astronauts were killed when a fire broke out on the launchpad. Subsequent flights put astronauts into orbit around first Earth and then the Moon, testing the equipment they would need to land on the Moon.

Moon walking

By 1969, the Apollo project was ready. On July 16, *Apollo 11* blasted off from Cape Kennedy in Florida. Once in Moon orbit, the lunar module *Eagle* separated from the command module, taking Neil Armstrong and Buzz Aldrin down to the surface of the Moon. On July 20, at 10:56 p.m., Armstrong made history by walking on the Moon, followed shortly afterward by Aldrin.

Buzz Aldrin steps down from the *Eagle* onto the Moon.

What Next!

After the success of Apollo 11, five more manned missions landed on the Moon. The last was in 1972. Nobody has been there since.

Time Line

January 27, 1967
Apollo 1 catches fire on the launchpad, killing the three astronauts onboard

October 11, 1968
Apollo 7 makes manned flight around Earth

December 21, 1968
Apollo 8 makes first manned flight around the Moon

July 20, 1969
Apollo 11 makes first Moon landing

July 26, 1971
Apollo 15 sends a rover vehicle to explore the surface of the Moon

December 7, 1972
Apollo 17 makes final Apollo mission

The *Apollo 11* crew

Neil Armstrong (left), Edwin "Buzz" Aldrin (right), and Michael Collins (center), were all born in 1930. They trained as military pilots before becoming astronauts, making their first space flights in the Gemini program in 1966. While the other two astronauts descended to the Moon onboard the lunar module *Eagle*, Collins remained in orbit around the Moon onboard the Columbia command module.

GLOSSARY AND TIME LINE

Archeology
The study of the material remains of past civilizations.

Archipelago
Large group of islands.

Arctic Circle
Imaginary line around the North Pole that marks the limit of the region that experiences 24-hour darkness in midwinter. A similar line called the Antarctic Circle surrounds the South Pole.

Astrolabe
Instrument used by sailors to measure the height of the sun at noon, giving the ship's latitude.

Astronaut
American name for a person who travels in space. The Russian equivalent is a cosmonaut.

c.
Abbreviation for the Latin word circa, meaning about. It is used when an exact date is unknown and the date shown is approximate.

Caravan
Company of traders traveling together for safety across a desert or potentially hostile area with a train of pack animals, usually camels or horses.

Caravel
Ocean-going, square-rigged, three-masted ship developed by the Portuguese.

Catamaran
Yacht with two hulls.

Chronometer
Watch designed to be accurate in all climate conditions.

Circumnavigation
Journey made all the way around the world.

Colony
Region or country that is controlled by another country.

Commerce
Trade, or the buying or selling of goods on a large scale, usually for profit.

Continent
One of the seven great landmasses of the world: North America, South America, Europe, Africa, Asia, Australasia (Oceania), and Antarctica.

Culture
The way of life of a particular people or country, including their art, literature, and music.

c.1470 B.C. Egyptians sail to Punt	**1405** Zheng He starts the first of his seven voyages
c.475 B.C. Hanno sails down west coast of Africa	**1418** Henry the Navigator founds school at Sagres
c.330 B.C. Pytheas sails around Britain; visits Thule	**1486** Diogo Cão sails to Cape Cross in Namibia
c.200 B.C. Polynesians settle Tahiti	**1488** Bartolomeu Dias rounds Cape of Good Hope
138 B.C. Zhang Qian travels through central Asia	**1492** Christopher Columbus sails across Atlantic
A.D. 399 Faxian travels from China to India	**1497** Vasco da Gama opens up sea route to India; John Cabot sails to Newfoundland
A.D. 629 Xuanzang travels from China to India	**1499** Amerigo Vespucci sails along coast of Brazil
A.D. 921 Ibn Fadlan travels through central Asia	**1513** Núñez de Balboa sights the Pacific Ocean
c.1000 Leif Erikson sails to Vinland	**1519** Ferdinand Magellan sets out west from Europe
1253 William of Rubruck visits the Great Khan	**1521** Hernán Cortés seizes Aztec Empire
1271 Marco Polo sets out for China	**1522** Delcano completes first circumnavigation
1325 Ibn Battuta sets off from Tangier for Mecca	

Czar
The hereditary emperor or ruler of Russia. Also spelled tsar.

Empire
Many different lands and countries ruled over by one leader.

Equator
Imaginary line around Earth at an equal distance between the North and South Poles.

Frigate
Medium-sized warship of the 18th and 19th centuries.

Galleon
Large sailing ship used as a warship or merchant ship.

Geology
The study of the solid matter of Earth, including rocks and soil.

Headwaters
Streams that flow into one another to start a river.

Hydrography
The study of Earth's oceans, seas, and rivers.

Isthmus
Narrow strip of land connecting two larger areas of land.

Junk
Chinese sailing vessel with a flat bottom and square sails.

Ketch
Two-masted sailing vessel.

Knot
A speed of one nautical mile per hour. A nautical mile is equivalent to 6,076 feet (1.85 km).

Latitude
The distance north or south of the equator, measured in degrees.

Linguist
Person who studies languages and can usually read and write many different languages.

Log
Detailed record of a ship's voyage, updated every day or sometimes every hour.

Longitude
The distance east or west of an imaginary line that runs from the North to the South Pole through Greenwich in England, measured in degrees.

Magnetic South Pole
Place to which all compasses in the southern hemisphere point.

1528	Pánfilo de Narváez explores Florida
1533	Francisco Pizarro seizes Inca Empire
1535	Jacques Cartier searches for Northwest Passage
1541	Francis Xavier travels through Asia
1553	Richard Chancellor finds sea route to Russia
1554	Alvaro de Mendaña sails across the Pacific
1577	Francis Drake begins circumnavigation
1594	Willem Barents searches for Northeast Passage
1603	Samuel de Champlain explores Canada
1607	Luis Váez de Torres sails around New Guinea
1610	Henry Hudson discovers the Hudson Strait
1624	Antonio de Andrade crosses the Himalayas
1642	Abel Tasman sails around Australia
1661	Grueber and D'Orville visit Lhasa
1673	Louis Jolliet explores Mississippi
1674	William Dampier begins circumnavigation
1682	Cavelier de La Salle reaches Mississippi Delta
1725	Vitus Bering journeys to Siberia
1740	George Anson sets sail around the world
1766	John Byron completes circumnavigation; Louis-Antoine de Bougainville sets out to colonize South Pacific from France
1768	James Cook sets sail for the Pacific
1770	James Bruce discovers the source of the Blue Nile

Missionary
A person who travels to convert the local people to his or her religion.

Monastery
Place of residence of a religious order of monks.

Monohull
Yacht with a single hull.

Mutiny
Rebellion by seamen or soldiers against their commanding officers.

New World
Term used by Europeans to describe North America after they first visited it in the 16th century. Europe, Asia, and Africa became known as the Old World.

Nomads
People who move from place to place in search of food, water, and land for their animals to graze.

Northern hemisphere
The half of Earth that lies north of the equator.

North Pole
The northernmost point of Earth's axis of rotation, which lies in the center of Arctic Circle.

Northeast Passage
A route from the Atlantic Ocean around the north of Siberia into the Pacific Ocean.

Northwest Passage
A route from the Atlantic Ocean around the north of Canada and into the Pacific Ocean.

Oceanography
Study of the world's oceans and their physical, chemical, geological, and biological features.

Pack ice
Ice floating on the sea or ocean, packed together in huge sheets, found in the Arctic and Antarctic.

Padrão
Stone cross used by Portuguese navigators to mark their progress down the African coast.

Peninsula
Narrow strip of land surrounded by water on three sides.

Pilgrimage
Journey to a shrine or other sacred place, made by a pilgrim.

Polar
Relating to the North or South Poles.

Polar ice cap
Frozen sheet of ice that covers the area around the North and South Poles.

1785 Comte de La Pérouse explores the Pacific

1796 Mungo Park reaches the Niger

1804 Lewis and Clark cross North America

1812 Johann Ludwig Burckhardt visits Petra

1828 Charles Sturt begins to map Australian rivers; René Caillié enters Timbuktu

1830 Richard Lander follows the Niger to the sea

1835 Charles Darwin visits the Galápagos Islands

1838 Charles Wilkes leads scientific expedition

1841 Edward Eyre crosses Australia east–west; David Livingstone begins to explore Africa

1842 John Frémont starts to open up western United States

1850 Heinrich Barth sets out across the Sahara

1858 Richard Burton first sees Lake Tanganyika

1860 Burke and Wills cross Australia south–north

1861 John Stuart raises British flag near Darwin

1862 John Speke discovers the source of the Nile

1871 Livingstone and Henry Stanley meet at Ujiji; Charles Hall reaches north shore of Greenland

1872 HMS *Challenger* explores the world's oceans

1876 Henry Stanley starts to explore the Congo

1879 Adolf Nordenskiöld sails Northeast Passage

1890 Sven Hedin sets out for central Asia

1893 Fridtjof Nansen begins journey on the *Fram*; Mary Kingsley first sets out for West Africa

Press gang
Group of usually armed men who force civilians to join the army or navy.

Quadrant
Navigation instrument used by sailors to calculate the angle of a star so that they can work out a ship's latitude. The quadrant was replaced in the 18th century by the octant, and then the more accurate sextant.

Schooner
Sailing vessel with at least two masts. All the lower sails on a schooner are rigged from front to back.

Scurvy
Disease caused by a lack of vitamin C, which often used to affect sailors when they did not eat fresh fruit or vegetables on long voyages.

Scuttle
To deliberately sink a ship to stop it from falling into enemy hands.

Silk Road
Ancient trade route linking China through central Asia and the Middle East to the Mediterranean and on to Europe.

Sloop
A single-masted sailing vessel.

Source
The spring or headwaters from which a river begins.

Southern hemisphere
The half of Earth that lies south of the equator.

South Pole
Southernmost point of Earth's axis of rotation, which lies in Antarctica.

Square-rigged
Ship rigged with square or rectangular sails, often hanging from a solid beam.

Storeship
A ship used purely to store supplies for an expedition.

Strait
Narrow channel of water between two seas or oceans.

Trade
The process of buying and selling goods.

Treasure ship
Galleon or other large ship used to carry gold, silver, and other precious goods.

Trimaran
Yacht with three hulls, usually with a main hull flanked by two smaller hulls.

1895	Joshua Slocum sets out on solo voyage around the world
1899	Gertrude Bell starts to explore Middle East
1900	Aurel Stein starts to explore western China
1906	Roald Amundsen navigates Northwest Passage
1909	Peary and Henson reach North Pole
1911	Roald Amundsen reaches South Pole
1927	Freya Stark travels through Arabian desert
1930	Bertram Thomas crosses Empty Quarter; Beebe and Barton make their first descent in the bathysphere in the waters off Bermuda
1943	Jacques Cousteau invents the aqualung
1945	Wilfred Thesiger explores the Empty Quarter
1947	Thor Heyerdahl crosses Pacific on *Kon-Tiki*
1953	Hillary and Tenzing climb Everest
1957	USSR launches first satellite, *Sputnik 1*
1958	Vivian Fuchs crosses Antarctica
1960	*Trieste* descends to bottom of Mariana Trench
1961	Yuri Gagarin is first man in space
1967	Francis Chichester completes first solo, one-stop circumnavigation
1969	Robin Knox–Johnston completes first solo, nonstop circumnavigation; Armstrong and Aldrin walk on the Moon
2008	Francis Joyon sets new solo record of 57 days for solo, nonstop circumnavigation

INDEX

A

Aborigines 157, 159, 160
Adams, William 84
Africa 12–13, 25, 33,
    36–44, 57, 165–89
Alaska 49, 50, 72, 151
Aldrin, Buzz 215
Aleutian Islands 50, 151
Alexandria 24
Amazon 69, 134–35
Americas 113–37
Amerike, Richard 66
Amundsen, R. 78–79, 198–99
Andrade, Antonio de 47
Andrée, Salomon 193
Anson, George 98, 100
Antarctica 104, 105, 145,
    148–49, 196–203
Apollo program 214–15
aqualung 208, 209
Arabia 25, 33, 54–59
Arawaks 63
Arctic 76–79, 192–95
Arctic Ocean 72, 74, 79,
    81, 192
Armstrong, Neil 215
Ascension Island 97, 107
Asia 16–18, 26, 30, 35–59,
    88–91
astrolabe 43
Atlantic Ocean 20, 22, 42, 66,
    69, 72, 88, 93, 108
Aurel Stein, Sir Marc 53
Australia 97, 103, 104, 107,
    144–45, 147, 152–53,
    155–61
Aztecs 118–19

B

Balboa, Núñez de 116, 120
ballooning 193
Banks, Joseph 147, 152, 166
Barents, Willem 81
Barth, Heinrich 172–73
Barton, Otis 206
Bass, George 156
Bates, Henry 134, 135
bathyscaphe 207
bathysphere 206
bearing dial 21
Bedouin 55, 56, 57, 59
Beebe, William 206
Beijing 30, 31, 32, 33
Bell, Gertrude 58, 59
Bering Sea 72, 79, 83, 151
Bering, Vitus 48–51, 151
Bonpland, Aimé 134
Borchgrevink, C. 196–97
Botany Bay 147, 152–53, 155
Bougainville, L.-A. de 102
Brassey, Thomas 107
Brazil 41, 68–69, 106
Brett, Piercy 99
Britain 14–15, 124
Bruce, James 174–75
Buddhism 18–19, 26, 53
Burckhardt, J. L. 54–55
Burke, Robert 158–59
Burton, R. 55, 176–77, 179
Byron, John 100–101

C

Cabeza de Vaca, Álvar 117
Cabot, John 66–67
Cabral, Pedro 41, 68, 69
Cadamosto, Alvise da 44
Caillié, René 170–71
Calicut, India 42, 43
California 132, 133
camels 159, 170
Cameroon, Mount 12, 189
Canada 21, 67, 72
canoes 125, 140
Cão, Diogo 38, 39
Cape Horn 93, 98, 109, 110
Cape of Good Hope 40, 41, 42,
    104, 110
Cape Verde Islands 44, 106
caravel 37, 62, 69
Caribbean 68, 114–15
Carson, Kit 133
Carthage 12, 13
Cartier, Jacques 124–25
Carvalho, João Lopes 90, 91
Caspian Sea 29
Cavendish, Thomas 96
Central America 115, 116
Ceuta, Morocco 36, 37
Challenger 204–205
Challenger Deep 207
Champlain, Samuel de 125
Chancellor, Richard 80, 81
Charlevoix, P. de 128, 129
Chelyuskin, Semion 51
Chichester, Francis 108–9
China 16–19, 26–27, 30–33,
    37, 46, 47, 52
Chirikov, Alexei 50, 51
chronometer 149
Chukchi people 83
Clapperton, Hugh 168
Clark, William 130–31
Collins, Michael 215

Columbus, Christopher 39, 61,
    62–66, 68, 113–15
Commerçon, Philibert 103
compass 33
Congo 187
Congo River 38, 39, 186–87
Cook, James 146–51, 196
Coronado, Vásquez de 123
Corps of Discovery 130
Cortés, Hernán 118–19
Cousteau, Jacques 208–209
Cuba 63, 115, 118

D E

Dampier, William 96
Darwin, Charles 135–37
Davis, John 73
Delcano, Juan 90, 91
Denham, Dixon 168, 169
Dias, Bartolomeu 40–42
Doughty, Charles 55
Drake, Francis 92–95
Dutch East Indies 103, 145
Easter Island 140–41, 155
Egyptians 9, 10–11, 13
Elizabeth I, Queen 92, 93
Elmina, Ghana 37, 38, 39
Empty Quarter 56–57
Endeavour 147, 152
Erikson, Leif 20, 21
Erik the Red 21
Ethiopia 56
Everest, Mount 210–11
Eyre, Edward 156, 157

F

Faeroe Islands 21, 22, 23
Falkland Islands 100, 101

Faxian 18, 19
Fiji 140, 145
Flinders, Matthew 156
Florida 70, 116, 117, 122
Francis I of France 70
Franklin, Sir John 76–78
Frémont, John 132
Frobisher, Martin 72, 73
Fuchs, Vivian 201

G

Gagarin, Yuri 212, 213
Galápagos Islands 135–37
Gama, Vasco da 41, 42–43
Gambia River 44, 45
Genghis Khan 28, 29
Giovanni da Pian del
    Carpine 28, 29
Gobi Desert 31, 52
Goes, Bento de 46, 47
gold 63, 73, 92, 95, 113, 120,
    122–23
Golden Hind 92, 93, 94–95
Gonçalves, Lopo 37
Grant, James 178–79
Great Barrier Reef 103, 147
Great Northern Expedition
    50–52
Great Salt Lake 133
Greeks 9, 14–15
Greenland 20–23, 74, 192
Grueber, John 47
Guam 89

H

Hall, Charles 192
Hanno 12–13
Harrison, James 149

Hatshepsut, Queen 10, 11
Hawaii 104, 140, 150, 151
Hawkins, John 93
Hedin, Sven 52, 53
Henry VII of England 67
Henry the Navigator 36–37
Henson, Matthew 195
Heyerdahl, Thor 162–63
Hillary, Edmund 210–11
Himalayas 18, 47, 210–11
Hispaniola 63, 114, 115
Hudson, Henry 74–75
Hudson Bay 73, 75
Humboldt, A. von 134

I

Ibn Battuta 24–27
Ibn Fadlan 26
Iceland 15, 21, 22, 23
Ieyasu, Tokugawa 84
Igbo people 169
Incas 120, 163
India 18–19, 26, 33, 35,
    37–43, 46, 47
Indian Ocean 33, 41, 42, 43,
    103, 104
Indonesia 18, 88, 140
Ingstad, Helge 21
Inuit 21, 50, 72, 78, 192
Iraq 25, 56, 57, 58, 59
Ivan the Terrible 80

J

Japan 46, 47, 62, 84–85
Jefferson, Thomas 130
Jesuits 46, 47, 84
João II of Portugal 39, 40
Jolliet, Louis 126

K

Kamchatka Peninsula 48, 49
Karakorum 28, 29
Karlsefni, Thorfinn 21
Kenya 25, 42, 56
King William Island 77, 78
Kingsley, Mary 188–89
Knox-Johnston, Robin 110
Kon-Tiki expedition 162–63
Kublai Khan 30, 31
Küyük, Great Khan 28, 29

L

La Condamine, C-M. de 134
La Pérouse, Comte 154–55
La Salle, C. de 126, 129
Lander, Richard & John 169
latitude 43, 149
Leopold II of Belgium 187
Lewis, Meriwether 130–31
Lhasa, Tibet 47, 52
Lisbon 37, 62
Livingstone, David 180–85
longitude 43, 149
Louis IX of France 28
Louisiana 127

M

Macao 98, 99
MacArthur, Ellen 110, 111
Mactan, Battle of 88, 89
Magellan, Ferdinand 88–91
Magellan Straits 88–90, 93, 106
Maldives 26
Mali 27, 1¡66, 167
Manuel I of Portugal 42
Maoris 140

maps 36, 52, 69
Marquette, Jacques 126
Marsh Arabs 57
Mawson, Douglas 201
McClintock, Francis 77
Mecca 24–25, 54, 55
Mediterranean 12, 13, 15
Mendaña, Alvaro de 142
Mercator, Gerardus 69
Mexico 118–19, 133
Middle East 27, 28, 59
Ming Dynasty 32–33
missionaries 29, 35, 46–47, 180
Mississippi River 122, 126–27, 130
Missouri River 129, 130
Moctezuma II 119
Mombasa, Kenya 25, 42
Mongols 28–29, 30, 32
Moon 214–15
Murray, John 204–205
Muscovy Company 74, 80
Muslims 24–27, 29, 42, 54, 59, 166, 170

N O

Nansen, Fridtjof 192, 193
navigation 21, 33, 36, 37, 43, 141, 149
Newfoundland 21, 67, 71
New Guinea 143, 145
New Holland 86
New World 69, 112–37
New York Bay 71, 75
New Zealand 33, 140, 145, 146
Niger River 166–69, 171
Nile River 10, 11, 24, 25
        source of 174–79, 182

Nordenskiöld, Adolf 82–83
Norsemen 9, 20–23
North America 20–21, 67, 70, 116, 122–29, 150
North Pole 192–95
Northeast Passage 74–75, 80–83
northern lights 14, 15
Northwest Passage 72–79, 124, 150–51
oceans 204–209
Ojeda, Alonso de 68
Oregon 104, 105, 132, 151
Orville, Albert d' 47
Oudney, Walter 168, 169

P Q

Pacific islands 101, 102, 140–43, 149, 162
Pacific Ocean 72, 89–94, 96, 97, 98, 116, 139–43
Park, Mungo 166–67
Peary, Robert 194–95, 199
Perry, Matthew 84, 85
Persia 25, 28, 59
Peru 120
Peter the Great 48, 49
Petra, Jordan 54, 55
Philippines 88, 89, 91
Phoenicians 9, 12–13
Pinzón, Vicente 68, 69
pirates 70, 72, 90, 92, 96–97
Pizarro, Francisco 120–21
Polo, Marco 30–31
Polynesia 139–41, 162–63
Ponce de León, J. 116–17
porcelain 33
Portuguese 35–45, 84, 114

press gangs 98
Puerto Rico 116, 117
Punt 10–11
purple dye 13
Pytheas 14–15
quadrant 43
Québec 124, 125, 128
Quirós, Pedro de 143

R

rafts 162–63
Raleigh, Sir Walter 124
Red Sea 10, 11, 24, 25
Roanoke Island 124
Rocky Mountains 130–33
Ross, Sir James 196
Russia 26, 28, 30, 35, 48–51, 74, 80

S

Sacsahuamán fortress 121
Sahara 170–73
St. Lawrence River 124–25
San Francisco 79, 93
San Salvador 62, 65
Santo Domingo 115
scientists 134–35, 146, 197, 204–205
Scott, Robert 198–99
Selkirk, Alexander 97
Shackleton, Ernest 200–203
shoguns 84, 85
Siberia 35, 48–51, 81–83
Silk Road 17, 18, 26, 35, 37, 52–53
Sioux people 129
slave trade 38, 93, 168, 169, 180, 182–83

Slocum, Joshua 106–107
Solander, Daniel 147, 152
Solomon Islands 142, 143
Soto, Hernando de 122
South America 68, 69, 98, 114
South Pole 78, 149, 198–203
South Seas 102–105, 142–43, 146–47
Southeast Asia 26, 32, 33
Southern Ocean 41
space 212–15
Spain 27, 92, 98, 114–23
Speke, John Hanning 176–79
Spice Islands 90, 91, 93
spice trade 42, 43, 91
Spitsbergen 80, 81
Spruce, Richard 135
Sputnik 1 213
Sri Lanka 27, 33, 46, 47
Stanley, Henry 178, 183–87
Stark, Freya 58, 59
stick charts 141
Stuart, John 160–61
Sturt, Charles 156, 157
Suez Canal 78, 107
Syria 24, 54, 55, 58, 59

T

Tahiti 102, 140, 146, 149
Taklimakan Desert 52, 53
Tana, Lake 174, 175
Tanganyika, Lake 176, 177, 182
Tasman, Abel 144–45
Tasmania 145, 156
Tenochtitlán 118, 119
Tenzing Norgay 210–11
Texas 117

Thesiger, Wilfred 56, 57
Thomas, Bertram 56
Thule 14, 15
Tibet 47, 52
Tierra del Fuego 104, 105
Timbuktu 166–67, 171, 173
tobacco 63
Tordesillas, Treaty of 114
Torres, Luis Váez de 143
Tuareg nomads 171, 173

U V W

United States 84, 85, 132
Verrazano, G. da 70–71
Vespucci, Amerigo 68, 69
Victoria, Lake 177–79, 186
Vikings 20–23
Vincennes 105
Vinland 20, 21
Vostok 1 213
Wallace, Alfred 135
West Indies 63, 93
Western Sea 128–29
whales 23, 111
Wilkes, Charles 104–105
William of Rubruck 28, 29
Wills, William John 158–59

X Y Z

Xavier, St Francis 46, 47
Xuanzang 19
Yaqui people 117
Yongle, Emperor 32, 33
Yue-chi tribe 16
Zambezi River 180, 181, 183
Zhang Qian 16–17
Zheng He 32–33

ACKNOWLEDGMENTS

Artwork supplied by Martin McKenna, Michael Welply, and Mike White, and through Linden Artists by Adam Hook, Francis Phillipps, and Clive Spong.

Photo credits:
b = bottom, t = top, r = right, l = left, c = center

Cover images:
Front: br Laurie Chamberlain/CORBIS, bc CORBIS, bl Tetra Images/CORBIS, c Bert Leidmann/zefa/CORBIS, tr Morton Beebe/CORBIS, tc Ralph A. Clevenger/CORBIS, tl Matthew McKee; Eye Ubiquitous/CORBIS.
Back: bl Steven Vidler/Eurasia Press/CORBIS, bc Jeremy Horner/CORBIS, tl Historical Picture Archive/CORBIS, tr Douglas Pearson/CORBIS.
Spine: Gordon R. Gainer/CORBIS.

1 Shilo Long/Dreamstime.com, 2-3 Alexander Potapov/Dreamstime.com, 6tr Pilar Echeverria/Dreamstime.com, 6b Bryan Busovicki/istockphoto, 6-7 Martin Brown/Dreamstime.com 7t NASA, 7cr NASA, 7b Burillier 7br Robb Cox/istockphoto.com, 8-9 Keren Su/CORBIS, 10-11 Vladimir Korostyshevskiy/Dreamstime.com, 10t Andrew Kershaw/Dreamstime.com, 10b Michał Kram/Dreamstime.com, 12-13 BishkekRocks, 12b Bettmann/CORBIS, 15t Deborah Benbrook/Dreamstime.com, 15b Matthias Kabel, 17 Werner Forman/CORBIS, 18-19 Simon Gurney/Dreamstime.com, 18b Elena Pokrovskaya/Dreamstime.com, 19b Ryszard Laskowski/Dreamstime.com, 20t Denise Kappa/istockphoto, 21t Erik Torpegaard, 21b Dylan Kereluk/creativecommons.org, 22-23 Olof Ekström, 22 Feng Yu/Dreamstime.com, 23 Darja Vorontsova/Dreamstime.com, 24-25 Kazuyoshi Nomachi/Corbis, 24b Pavel Bortel/Dreamstime.com, 25t Stefanie Van Der Vinden/Dreamstime.com, 26-27 Liu Liqun/Corbis, 26b Nasrulla Adnan/Dreamstime.com, 27t Monika Adamczyk/Dreamstime.com, 28t Bettmann/CORBIS, 29t Hamid Sardar/Corbis, 31t Hulton-Deutsch Collection/CORBIS, 32-33 Robert Churchill/iStockphoto, 33t Christopher Elwell/Dreamstime.com, 34-35 Krause, Johansen/Archivo Iconografico, SA/Corbis, 36-37 Archivo Iconografico, S.A./CORBIS, 36t Corbis, 37t The Art Archive/Corbis, 40 Celso Pupo Rodrigues/Dreamstime.com, 41 Krause, Johansen/Archivo Iconografico, SA/Corbis, 42-43 John Van Hasselt/CORBIS SYGMA, 42b Bettmann/CORBIS , 43t Norbert Speicher/istockphoto, 44 Sascha Dunkhorst/Dreamstime.com, 45t Gianni Dagli Orti/CORBIS, 45b Juan jose Gutierrez barrow/Dreamstime.com, 46t Santa Casa de Misericórdia de Lisboa/ Museu de São Roque, Lisbon, Portugal, 46b Arko Datta/Reuters/Corbis, 47b Keith Yong/Dreamstime.com, 48-49 NASA, 48b Bettmann/CORBIS, 49t PoodlesRock/Corbis, 50b National Maritime Museum, London, 51t Tatiana Edrenkina/Dreamstime.com, 51b Daniel J. Cox/Corbis, 52-53 Shilo Long/Dreamstime.com, 52b Bettmann/CORBIS, 53t Steve Estvanik/Dreamstime.com, 54-55 Adeeb Atwan/Dreamstime.com, 55t Bettmann/CORBIS, 55b George Steinmetz/Corbis, 56t Bettmann/Corbis, 56b Rama/Wikipedia ShareAlike, 57t Nik Wheeler/CORBIS, 59t Valery Shanin/Dreamstime.com, 59b Hulton-Deutsch Collection/CORBIS, 60-61 Pierre Colombel/CORBIS, 62l Bettmann/CORBIS, 63t Tradkelly/Dreamstime.com, 64t Library of Congress, 65t Dmitriy Norov/Dreamstime.com, 66-67 Christopher Howey/Dreamstime.com, 66t Bettmann/CORBIS, 66b David Hughes/Dreamstime.com, 67t John Farmar; Cordaiy Photo Library Ltd./CORBIS, 68-69 Stapleton Collection/Corbis, 68b NASA, 70b Bettmann/CORBIS, 71t Marianne Venegoni/Dreamstime.com, 71b Nina Sosnicka /Dreamstime.com, 71-72 Andrew Buckin/Dreamstime.com, 72b Staffan Widstrand/CORBIS, 73t Diego Barucco/Dreamstime.com, 75t Maureen Plainfield/Dreamstime.com, 75b Michael Nicholson/CORBIS, 76 US Library of Congress, 77t Brian0918/Wikipedia Commons, 78-79 Alexander Potapov/Dreamstime.com, 78b Layne Kennedy/CORBIS, 79b Paul A. Souders/CORBIS, 80-81 Pascaline Daniel/Dreamstime.com, 81t Stapleton Collection/Corbis, 81b Anthony Hathaway/Dreamstime.com, 83 Natalie Fobes/CORBIS, 84-85 Koi88/Dreamstime.com, 85b Asian Art & Archaeology, Inc./CORBIS, 86-87 National Gallery, London/CORBIS, 88-89 Historical Picture Archive/CORBIS, 89 Rodrigo roy a Boncato/Dreamstime.com, 91 Frans Lemmens/zefa/Corbis, 92-93 Joel W. Rogers/CORBIS, 93b Baldwin H. Ward & Kathryn C. Ward/CORBIS, 94t The Robert H. Gore, Jr. Numismatic Collection, 95 Burillier, 96-97 Susinder/Dreamstime.com, 96b Bettmann/CORBIS, 97b Andy Rouse/Corbis, 98b Joe Ho/istockphoto, 99b Dmitriy Murashko/Dreamstime.com, 101 Jeff Goldman/Dreamstime.com, 102-103 Owen Franken/CORBIS, 102b Leonard de Selva/CORBIS, 103t Richard Ling/Wikipedia ShareAlike, 104-105 Alexander Hafemann/istockphoto.com, 104b NOAA, 105t Grigory Kubatyan/Dreamstime.com, 105b Naval Art Collection, Washington, D.C., 107t Michael Maslan Historic Photographs/CORBIS, 108-109 Bettmann/CORBIS, 108t Chichester Archive/PPL, 109t Chichester Archive/PPL, 109b Ted Spiegel/CORBIS, 110-111 MOUSIS FRANCOIS/CORBIS SYGMA, 110b PPL Archive, 111b Brett Atkins/Dreamstime.com 112-113 Darrell Gulin/CORBIS, 116t Bettmann/CORBIS, 117b Sergey Ivanov/Dreamstime.com, 118-119 Charles & Josette Lenars/CORBIS, 119 The Art Archive/Corbis, 120-121 Bryan Busovicki/istockphoto, 120t Bettmann/CORBIS, 120b Carlos Santa Maria | Agency: Dreamstime.com, 121 Håkan Svensson, 123t Tom Bean/CORBIS, 123b Library of Congress, 124-125 Douglas Allen/istockphoto, 125b Burstein Collection/CORBIS, 126t Bettmann/CORBIS, 126b Bettmann/CORBIS, 127t CORBIS, 127b NASA, 128t Karl Bodmer, 129t Scott T. Smith/CORBIS, 130-131 Martin Brown/dreamstime.com, 130b Independence National Historical Park, 131t Smithsonian American Art Museum, 131b Michael Thompson/Dreamstime.com, 133t Library of Congress, 133b Remarsh/Dreamstime.com, 134-135 istockphoto, 135r Mark Kostich/istockphoto, 136-137 Erik Reis/Dreamstime.com, 136t Nikolay Okhitin/Dreamstime.com, 136c The Complete Work of Charles Darwin Online, 136b Bobby Deal/Dreamstime.com, 137b Robyn Mackenzie/Dreamstime.com, 138-139 Ron Sumners/Dreamstime.com, 140b Paul Chinn/San Francisco Chronicle/Corbis, 141t Jose Tejo/Dreamstime.com, 142t Michael C. Rockefeller Memorial Collection, 142-143 Bernard Breton/Dreamstime.com, 145b The Gallery Collection/Corbis, 146-147 Michael Willis/istockphoto, 146l National Archive of Canada, 147t Adam Booth/istockphoto.com, 147b Natural History Museum London, 148-149 Alexander Putaya/Dreamstime.com, 148 Museum of History and Industry/CORBIS, 149t Stapleton Collection/Corbis, 150-151 Jeanne Hatch/istockphoto.com, 150l Oksanaphoto/Dreamstime.com, 151t Martyn Unsworth/istockphoto.com, 152l Pilar Echeverria/Dreamstime.com, 153t Michael C. Rockefeller Memorial Collection, 153b Wieslaw Fila/Dreamstime.com, 155b The Gallery Collection/Corbis, 156-157 Robb Cox/istockphoto.com, 157t Penny Tweedie/Corbis, 158-159 Chris Hellier/CORBIS, 159t Antonela Magzan/Dreamstime.com, 160t John McDouall Stuart Society, 161t John McDouall Stuart Society, 162-163 Kon Tiki Museum, 162l Bettmann/CORBIS, 163t Pcphotos/Dreamstime.com, 163b Margita Braze/Dreamstime.com, 164-165 Vladimir Kindrachov/Dreamstime.com, 166-167 Remi Benali/Corbis, 167t Alan Tobey/istockphoto.com, 169 Christie's Images/CORBIS, 170-171 François De Ribaucourt/Dreamstime.com, 170b Kornelis Bakker/istockphoto.com, 171t Wolfgang Kaehler/CORBIS, 173t Alan Tobey/istockphoto, 174-175 Torleif Svensson/CORBIS, 174t Krause, Johansen/Archivo Iconografico, SA/Corbis, 174b Jacob Eliosoff, 176-177 Michael S. Lewis/CORBIS, 176t Stapleton Collection/Corbis, 177t Luc Sesselle/ Dreamstime.com, 178t Stapleton Collection/Corbis, 179t Klaas Lingbeek- van Kranen/istockphoto, 179b Liz Leyden/istockphoto, 180b Hulton archive/istockphoto.com, 182-183 Bettmann/CORBIS, 182b Nik Wheeler/CORBIS, 184t Natalia Siverina/Dreamstime.com, 184br Svetlana Larina/Dreamstime.com, 184-185t Peter Gustafson/Dreamstime.com, 184-185b Elena Schweitzer/Dreamstime.com, 185t Natalia Siverina/Dreamstime.com, 186t Smithsonian Institution, 187t Hulton-Deutsch Collection/CORBIS, 188-189 Philippe Giraud/Goodlook/Corbis, 189t Lindsay Hebberd/CORBIS, 189b Chris Fourie/Dreamstime.com, 190-191 Bernard Breton/Dreamstime.com, 192-193 Tomasz Resiak/istockphoto, 192t US Library of Congress, 192b US Library of Congress, 193t US Library of Congress, 194-195 Stapleton Collection/Corbis, 194t US Library of Congress, 195t US Library of Congress, 196b Bettmann/CORBIS, 197t Ian Stevens, 198t Hulton-Deutsch Collection/CORBIS, 198b Bettmann/Corbis, 200l Underwood & Underwood/CORBIS, 200r US Library of Congress, 201b Morton Beebe/CORBIS, 202l Brad Sauter/Dreamstime.com, 202b Kai Hecker/Dreamstime.com, 203tl Vividpixels/Dreamstime.com, 203tr Kirsty Pargeter/Dreamstime.com, 203r Igor Terekhov/Dreamstime.com, 204t NOAA Photo Library, 205b istockphoto.com, 206-207 Dr. Steve Ross/NOAA, 206b Ralph White/CORBIS, 208-209 Matthias Weinrich/Dreamstime.com, 208b Doxa, 209b Simon Gurney/istockphoto.com, 210-211 Jose Fuente/Dreamstime.com, 210b Bettmann/CORBIS, 211t Peter Hazlett/Dreamstime.com, 211b Robert Churchill/istockphoto, 212-213 NASA, 214l NASA, 214-215t NASA, 214-215b NASA.